LIBRARY SUCCESS:

A Celebration of Library Innovation, Adaptation and Problem Solving

EDITED BY
DR. LESLIE EDMONDS HOLT, DR. GLEN HOLT, AND STRATTON LLOYD

FOREWORD

Every day, EBSCO Publishing has the pleasure to work with thousands of libraries and librarians around the world. Over the years, we have come to know them and have watched them nimbly adapt to the technical evolution from paper to CD-ROM to online services, the new demands of tech savvy users and the challenges of more complex curriculum integration and programmatic needs. We have seen firsthand how libraries have successfully deployed tools, techniques and processes to adapt and promote their services for the benefit of their patrons. We have been impressed.

Given the rapid pace of development and change in today's society, the time limits each of us face and the massive amount of information being published, effective information sharing has become imperative. With *Library Success: A Celebration of Library Innovation, Adaptation and Problem Solving*, we have attempted to develop an actionable reference tool targeting five important and challenging library management topics. Each topic is followed by several related success stories of work accomplished in North American libraries. Our goals in publishing this book are to celebrate the success of selected libraries and to facilitate information sharing among all libraries struggling with similar challenges.

I am delighted that we were able to work with Drs. Glen & Leslie Holt as, without their experience and guidance, the idea for this publication would not have become a reality. In order to increase the distribution and reach of *Library Success: A Celebration of Library Innovation, Adaptation and Problem Solving*, the stories are also being made available on our online Customer Success Center, www.ebscohost.com, where we will build off of this book's foundation and continue to foster library success through tools, resources, and additional success stories.

We at EBSCO Publishing are grateful to our library customers for the support they have shown us over the years. Let me take this opportunity to say 'thank you'. We hope that this publication proves useful to the library community and inspires more library success.

Tim Collins
President
EBSCO Publishing

Contents

LIBRARY SUCCESS:
A Celebration of Library Innovation, Adaptation and Problem Solving

EDITED BY
DR. LESLIE EDMONDS HOLT, DR. GLEN HOLT AND STRATTON LLOYD

Printed in the U.S.A

Cover and Book Design: Stephen Tierney
Illustrations: Will Harney

ATTAINING
SUCCESSFUL LIBRARIES

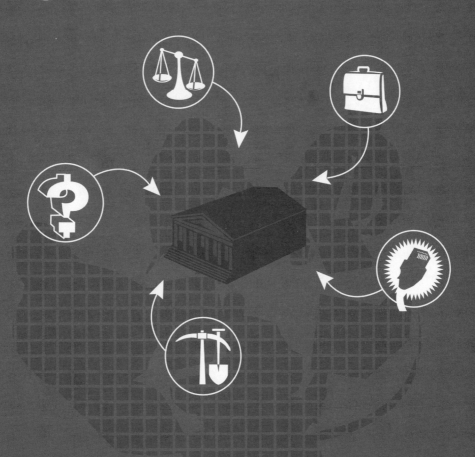

INTRODUCTION

This book is a key milestone in EBSCO Publishing's SUCCESSFUL LIBRARIES PROJECT. The project's mission is to assist, promote, and celebrate the successes of our customers as they improve the way they obtain and manage their resources and deliver their services. The principal feature of the project is getting successful innovators to share their stories with other librarians. These success stories demonstrate best practices that other librarians can adapt and implement to bring positive changes in their own organizations.

EBSCO has developed this initiative because our customers have told us they want it. During an extensive survey and feedback-gathering effort in 2005, EBSCO Publishing customers shared their greatest challenges. Forty-seven percent of respondents, reflecting academic, public, and school librarians, said "utilization," getting faculty, students, and patrons aware of and using the tools the library offers, was their greatest struggle. Another 36 percent reported funding, including convincing administrators of the importance of new resources, as their number one challenge. Time management and staff morale were also noted as key library challenges.

When asked what tools they would like to have for overcoming these challenges, 51 percent of respondents said they would like to see best practice examples: success stories from other libraries about how they innovated programs and services. Thirty-eight percent of respondents also wanted tools and advice on marketing the library's offerings. Thirty-two percent expressed interest in seeing industry trends and studies, while 30 percent wanted helpful resources regarding funding. Most importantly, our customers wanted tools and help that were actionable – easily replicated examples they could quickly apply at their own institutions.

The company's immediate response to requests for such information was to develop the EBSCO Customer Success Center, located on the company's website at www.ebscohost.com. There you will find over 200 free Success Tools encompassing such areas as:

- Funding
- Grant Writing
- Marketing
- Professional Development
- Library Assessment
- Special Event Planning

These unique tools are targeted to extend the access of your eResources, optimize research effectiveness, increase usage and usability, and help improve collaboration between administrators and end users. The Customer Success Center includes free access to the *Library, Information Science & Technology Abstracts* (LISTA) and *Teacher Reference Center* (TRC) databases, "How-Tos" for librarians, teachers, and students, and a growing repository of "success stories" with a wide range of best practice library examples. That collection includes downloadable PDF versions of all the stories in this volume, as well as many more.

Our company wants to ensure that you and your library have all the tools you need to excel in today's ever-challenging information age. If you are successful, EBSCO will be successful.

FOCUS ON CHANGING ISSUES

Decades ago, University of California President Clark Kerr wrote an article entitled, "The frantic race to remain contemporary."[1] In that essay, Kerr noted that rapid and dramatic shifts in technology, attitudes toward public funding, and a dramatic shift in values among U.S. citizens were having a powerful impact. These and other big changes meant that North American universities were caught in "the frantic race to remain contemporary." Not to change, not to participate in "the frantic race," meant that institutions stagnated or died.

Today's libraries are caught up in the same kind of frantic race. Libraries face economic, social and cultural changes to which they must respond. When we talked with our librarian customers, they told us that five changes in particular are causing them to continue running in "the frantic race to remain contemporary." These five areas are funding, technology, marketing, collaboration/partnership and measurement and planning of quality performance and impact. These five topics are those addressed in the change stories found in this volume.

Funding

The first of these changes is in funding. School boards and administrators, faced with stagnation and even declines in public revenues are striking libraries out of the "essential instruction unit" budget column and moving them to the "may be nice to have," "support" or "discretionary administration" funding lines. Universities, facing costs rising faster than inflation, respond by teaching both on-campus and distance-education courses that require no "library research" or just no "research," trimming serials subscriptions and staffing critical service points with student help rather than librarians. Public libraries cut back on service levels, trim new book budgets, defer facilities maintenance, delay technology and software purchases, eliminate staff positions or cut hours. Schools cut back on services to instructional staff and students, stop buying new computers and databases, count textbooks as library books and trim hours of discretionary media center or library operation.

Promoting enrollment in its 2005 pre-conference seminar, "Image is Everything: Making Partners and Money for Your Library," ALA's Library Administration and Management Association (LAMA) stated its rationale for attendance with these words:

> Never before has there been such a need for libraries of all kinds to be proactive with their marketing and fundraising efforts. Each type of library from the public, to the school, to the academic to the special library, [is…faced with] unique issues of image,… funding and economics.

> While there are models of libraries that are combining the efforts of marketing and fundraising/development, many more are not…due to a lack of understanding of how to initiate and integrate these functions.

> The issue with librarians often is not a lack of ability to do the work, it is a lack of knowledge, confidence, and understanding of what needs to be done and how they actually have the skills necessary to be successful.[2]

The urgent tone of this LAMA announcement is a good place to begin any discussion of fundraising. That's because, for most libraries, fundraising has moved from an occasional sideline to an ongoing necessity.

The different reasons that motivate libraries to raise funds only validates this sense of necessity. Libraries conduct fundraising to initiate programs, improve services, purchase materials and technology, erect new or remodel old buildings, and to gather endowments that will yield revenue to support general operations or specific, valued programs.

The type of library often shapes the fundraising effort. Because college and university libraries operate as high visibility campus symbols and meeting places, they are viewed as key components in ongoing institutional development programs. Only a few libraries, mostly on large and medium-size campuses, run their own discrete fundraising programs, or at least have their own fundraising staff working in collaboration with the institutional development office.

Most public libraries, with their historic taxpayer funding, operate their development programs through friends groups or by organizing charitable foundations. Moreover, most public libraries operate as departments or agencies of local or county government where elected and appointed officials define the ways that they can approach taxpayers and friends to ask for contributions.

Public and privately-funded schools have to deal with similar issues. Yet, in an age in which many educational systems are strapped for cash, school media specialists, staff and administrators find that grants from philanthropies, state and federal agencies, individual citizens and businesses are critical in trying out much-desired innovations, sustaining arts and athletic programs, and supporting imperative educational elements such as staff training, new library books and more computers.

Fundraising is now part of the library way of life.

Technology

The need to acquire new technology often forces professional librarians to seek new revenue sources. Library budgets would not be so tight if libraries of all kinds did not have to balance a demand for more new books, expensive serials, basic literacy tutoring, children's programs, adult programs, and community outreach to professors, teachers and classes, etc., with the demand for more, newer and faster computers and high speed wired and wireless Internet connections, computer, Internet and information literacy training, free telephone calls, free downloads of movies and music, and whatever else is this week's hot new Internet-based uploading or downloading novelty.

This balancing act demonstrates how libraries, which have functioned previously as historical and current repositories of information and knowledge, are part of the worldwide communications and processing technology shift that is transforming the world more than did the automobile, telegraph, radio, and television.

The administrator of one of the libraries whose story is featured in this book, Maryruth F. Glogowski, of Buffalo State College's Butler Library, explains the difference that computers and high speed digital collections have made on post-secondary education. In her online introduction to the library, Glogowski writes:

> …In 1995 members of the library staff…started the Buffalo State College Website in order to have a virtual space to deliver electronic information to our patrons. Since that time we have added more and more information on almost a daily basis.

We spend about $500,000 per year on subscriptions that are delivered through these pages: encyclopedias, indexes, and full-text articles from more than 36,000 journals. We hope that having access from any computer or wireless Web device, any time of the day or night helps our patrons to do their research more effectively.

…We have an array of new computers throughout the library to allow you to do research in our building. You can even bring in your laptop. We have wireless access and plugins for ethernet. Check the online catalog for the call numbers and then go up to the stacks for the latest academic books. We have the best of both worlds at Butler Library: real and virtual.[3]

Public libraries and school media centers are making similar transformations. Technology – which at a minimum is a combination of faster computers, quick and reliable operating software and high-speed computerized wired and wireless communication – is redefining library services by offering options that did not exist a decade ago.

Before the Internet revolution, a library could have a million annual visitors, mostly coming from within a few (or a few dozen) miles away. Now, the same library still has a million visitors, plus more than a million website hits per month, which amounts to 70,000 hits per day. Technology has made the possibility of cheap information ubiquitous.

Before, a library served constituents who entered its buildings. Now, it serves these and a host of virtual customers from its own locale, as well as from other states, regions and nations. Should a library serve only those who pay its tuition or its taxes or anyone who keys into its virtual site asking for help that the library can provide? Librarians now have to define the edges of their services, not just in practical but in existential ways.

Before, a library built its reputation through person-to-person relationships with on-site customers. Now, more and more library transactions begin and remain anonymous with their only identity an easily changeable website address. Professional librarians now have to decide which customer to serve first, the familiar face standing at the circulation desk or the anonymous reference question from a distant location.

Before, the ultimate service demand was for something definite: "a correct journal reference," "the most recent book," or help finding or obtaining a specific article via an Interlibrary loan. Now, customers still want these services – plus free or inexpensive downloadable full text documents, instantaneous reproduction of quality digital photographs, high-speed public computers, wireless access, the latest software – and staff who are even more proficient in using the Internet than the customers are in searching their own specialized knowledge areas.

Many libraries, including those that tell their success stories in this book, have used the new technology with grace and imagination to create myriad new service possibilities. One of those stories is that of MOREnet, a statewide network that helps all libraries in the State of Missouri. Cisco Systems, one of MOREnet's major vendors, summarizes the advantages of statewide connectivity:

The hallmark of world-class research and education is collaboration—connecting people and ideas in joint intellectual effort. Missouri's Research and Education Network,

MOREnet, provides exactly the kind of connection that today's researchers and educators need. As part of the University of Missouri System, MOREnet provides reliable Internet access and support services to Missouri's higher education and public schools K-12, public libraries, community networks, and state government organizations…

Without the collaborative efforts of MOREnet members, you'd need multiple networks to accomplish the same things," says Todd Krupa, MOREnet information officer. "With the MOREnet network, they can leverage the capabilities of a single, consolidated network and obtain access to services such as EBSCO at a better price than they could receive individually. Collaboration provides more resources for everybody.[4]

In MOREnet and in other libraries as well, new technology means new service options along with new costs and new decisions about whom and how to serve.

Marketing

Marketing is the tool that libraries use to announce and build demand for their services and programs. Marketing proclaims what libraries think is important about their business.

Marketing is especially important in the Internet Age because consumer markets have been fragmenting into pieces of the mass markets that once dominated. Evidence of this fragmentation can be seen in the existence of hundreds of television channels, the similar numbers of satellite radio broadcasts and other "wireless entertainment alternatives" and the millions of list-servs, wikis, blogs, and "my spaces" by which individuals are attempting to build like-interest communities around themselves and/or their particular professional and personal curiosities, concerns and enjoyments.

As a result of this fragmentation and the new ways in which entrepreneurs are gathering to serve those micro-markets, libraries, which always have played an intermediary role between their users and the information and reading material they want, find their traditional users and their non-users harder to reach. The first prerequisite of all successful 21st-century librarianship is getting the attention of current and potential users. Whether a library is promoting a specific service or program, mounting a campaign to attract more users or imaging itself as an irreplaceable service to the community, it needs to devote time, expertise and creativity to ensure that its marketing hits the desired target.

As libraries segment their marketing to deal with this fragmentation, they should pay special attention to all varieties of non-users. People who don't use libraries express lots of reasons for not thinking much about them. Non-users tell survey-takers that they don't need libraries; they don't have time to go to the library; that the library staff is unfriendly; the facilities are inconveniently located or have ill-timed hours – and/or that the Internet has everything they need anyway. The high quality marketing survey that Buffalo-Erie County completed in 1998 added another significant reason. "As a rule, library non-users are much less knowledgeable about information options than are users,"[5] the study noted. In short, lack of interest in libraries has a strong association with a lack of information about the economic, social, cultural and political issues that affect them.

Library users tell quite a different story. They say that their virtual and in-person library visits save time; they get needed help from library staff with their academic research and their homework; they get access to authors and programs that meet their specific interests and needs; they obtain information on products, services and companies which make them better students, citizens and consumers; they are delighted with library programs for their kids; and they see library use as a great bargain for the taxes or tuition that they pay to support library buildings, staff and virtual use and information sites.

In marketing terms, that means that libraries must change their image – from passive repositories of books, magazines and reference materials to proactive places and virtual centers that provide access to information, search skill instruction, learning communities, inspiration, and entertainment.

Howard F. McGinn, then dean of libraries at Clarion University and now dean of libraries at Seton Hall University, introduces his library marketing essay on the ALA website with this passage:

> The academic library, like most libraries, has a self-imposed image problem. The library, tradition says, must be perceived as a center for serious thought and contemplation…The librarians and staff who work in the libraries must be perceived as serious scholars… Herein lies the problem for a marketing person: how to bring customers into an environment that often chooses to present itself as a place where even life insurance salesmen would look like party animals.[6]

Following this humorous portrayal, McGinn concludes this paragraph optimistically by noting, "The good news is that the image can easily be changed. Marketing an academic library can be successful."

The Georgia Institute of Technology success story in this book provides one good example of how an academic library expressly set out to redefine its campus image. Its marketing tool was collaboration, that is, providing a venue for student groups to show their talents and display its rationale to new GIT freshmen. That participation in the orientation beginning in 2004 made library staff conscious of how the library could advertise its helpful programs and staff by serving as a social as well as an intellectual center. By positioning the library as a gathering place, as well as a research hub, the staff gained opportunities to talk with students about library services and their subject specialties. As the library built its reputation as a campus social center, it gained respect among students as a good place to turn for assistance in completing assignments and doing research.

No one can hold such high opinions of libraries without first being made aware of the products and services that they provide. Good opinions of libraries begin with good library marketing. Solid marketing is as integral to the success of a library as the quality of the services it provides to its users.

Partnership and Collaboration
Marketing to audiences already using the services of another institution or business is an inexpensive approach to growing a crop of new users. Co-marketing, however, is only one kind of tool that libraries have used among their usually numerous partnership and collaboration activities.

Library partnerships and collaborations (the terms are used interchangeably in this essay) take place when two or more institutions recognize that formal cooperation will accomplish their respective missions better than if they work alone. Partnerships involve shared action, a joint venture to achieve a specific end or the pursuit of similar interests. In short, well-structured partnerships help a library do its job better and improve the lives of its constituents.

Recent changes in government program requirements, shifting funding mandates from government agencies and private-sector funding authorities, networked computing, tight budgets, customer desire for improved or new services and library desire to provide for more or different types of users have encouraged the number of partnerships. Whether partnerships are developed for these reasons or inspired as part of some organizational initiative, they remain a powerful strategic tool to help libraries accomplish goals or make changes.

The success stories in this book tell what can happen when a library sets out systematically to use partnerships as a strategic tool to accomplish its mission. Starting half a decade ago, the Williamsburg (VA) Regional Library defined what partnership meant to the organization and then went on to set up and partner in 16 thriving community "marriages." The strategy yielded extraordinary benefits. One was the establishment of a library-operated, award-winning cancer information resource center operated with the Williamsburg Community Hospital. Another effort resulted in an ongoing partnership with the Williamsburg Community Schools that involves the library in new-teacher orientation, an annual survey that informs the library about what is needed by teachers and students, and staff involvement in school instruction that enriches students' education and contributes to their success.

Much like Williamsburg, the success stories concerning Wauconda (IL) and Tucson-Pima (AZ), show that partnerships can extend library influence well beyond the physical structure or what is reflected in the library's budget. The stories about college libraries partnering with faculty or student groups illustrate how libraries are affirming their continuing importance in institutional instructional life in the high technology Internet Age. Such stories show that partnerships are a "natural" for entrepreneurial librarians wanting change.

Performance Management and Evaluation

As libraries cope with tighter budgets, new technology waves, and increased customer expectations, an evermore influential accountability culture hits all not-for-profits including libraries.

The accountability culture's demands for specifics – and usually statistical specifics – are now required business considerations. Grant reviewers to government institutions are looking for documented "proof" about how libraries are performing, how they are addressing customer needs, and how libraries are measuring their success.

The success stories in the performance and evaluation section of this volume provide wonderful illustrations of how libraries have used applied research and study to improve the quality of their programs and services. The Fort Worth Public Library, for example, used PLA's *Planning for Results* mechanisms to create a comprehensive roadmap of needed technology enhancements to make user experiences more positive.

King County (WA) Public Library went a step further. First, the King County Library's Discovery Team organized a statistically significant customer survey that reached 27 percent of all its users. Second, the library then initiated a Patron Experience Transformation Project. In that phase of study, they hired two different consulting firms and included 80 staff members. From these steps came the writing of the King County Library System Strategic Blueprint which is now being operationalized.

The accountability culture has a legal as well as a philosophical basis. The greatest push for accountability and quantifying outcomes for all libraries comes from a specific law. In 1993 the Federal Government passed the Government Performance and Results Act (GPRA)[7]. Addressing its constituent libraries and museums, the Institute of Museum and Library Services summarizes the effect of the law this way:

This law requires every government agency to establish specific performance goals for each of its programs, preferably with performance indicators stated in objective, quantifiable, and measurable terms. Agencies must report on their level of achievement in reaching these goals on an annual basis. The effects of GPRA are also trickling down to state and local government agencies that are using the lead of the federal government to require evidence that all public dollars are well spent.

This is not just a government issue. A similar emphasis on accountability is being incorporated into funding guidelines for most major foundations. From all sides, museums and libraries a receiving a clear message. If they are to compete for both public and private funds in an accountability environment, they must develop evaluation practices that provide the most compelling picture of the impact of their services.[8]

The passage of GPRA thus forms a legal landmark in changing the way that school, university and public libraries must measure their successful performance and their impact. Libraries that receive federal money must comply with the law and in the most objective terms set up and meet outcome and performance goals. At the same time, most libraries find that non-federal granting and gifting agencies –and even wealthy individuals – increasingly require the same kind of statistical measures in proposals, work statements and project reports that they receive.

With or without legislation similar to the Federal GPRA, state and local governments, including school boards, library boards, and state university boards of regents request similar outcome and impact measurements. Furthermore, foundations and even some individual donors who reserve the potential to provide significant donations, want a close accounting of how their money is spent and the results it produces. Financial auditors and accountants, meanwhile, push for higher standards from the expenditure side of library operations. In the age of accountability, libraries are being told that if they want the money, they must justify its good use and high impact by practicing transparency in their allocations and accounting and positive outcomes in their expenditures.

Focus on Tools for Change

As we have written and assembled the various pieces of this book, we have tried to make it useful in practical ways.

The introductory essays in this book and the five case studies in each section focus on how libraries change successfully. In varied kinds of settings, libraries succeed through planned organizational change that transforms best practices into common practices. The anticipated outcome of such changes, whether stated implicitly or explicitly, is to improve the way that a particular library, information department or media center uses its resources to create, innovate or deliver a service that meets the needs of one or several of its constituencies.

Another reason for choosing the stories presented here is that we believe they represent replicable successful steps in developing best practices in the never-ending quest to achieve great libraries. The case studies provide credible foundations for planned action in many different areas of library operations. Our goal is to highlight in short reviews, the basic challenge, solution, and benefits of each story, to make each success as replicable as possible. A short bibliograpy and worksheet follow each chapter to help you get started in assessing the potential of adapting the innovation to your own institution.

As we began to collect case study examples, it became apparent that there was a great deal of the similarity in the issues that librarians face as they plan and carry out their innovations. We suggest that different types of libraries can and should learn from each other. This book, therefore includes stories from university, public and school libraries from throughout North America. We know that much "silo thinking" exists in the library community. This book suggests that there are rich rewards that come to those who look for best practices beyond the type of library in which they work.

In all the case studies, you will observe that library change is not serendipitous but self conscious. Library change happens when a "bright idea" motivated by perceived need appears on the operational horizon and is implemented when that idea is refined by planning, resourcing, and strategizing. The goal always is the same: To make some aspect of the library operation work better in order to improve or extend library services to individuals, families, groups and society generally, and, at the same time, to move ever closer to the ideal of becoming a great library. Within this ideal network, every case study is a potential action model. We hope that one or more of the case studies in this book will serve as an action model for you and your colleagues. And if you would like to share your organization's own success, visit the EBSCO Publishing Customer Success Center at www.ebscohost.com to add your story to our online repository.

Endnotes

[1] Robert S. Morrison, *The contemporary university: USA* (Boston: Houghton Mifflin, 1966).

[2] American Library Association: Library Administration and Management Association, "Image is everything: Making partners and money for your library" [Announcement of seminar], 4 May 2006 <http://www.ala.org/lama/lamaprofdev/lamaregionalinst/lamareginstlist/imageeverything.htm>.

[3] *E.H. Butler Library Home Page* (Buffalo State College) 4 May 2006 <http://www.buffalostate.edu/library/about/welcome.asp>.

[4] "MOREnet: Providing Statewide Connection for Missouri's Educators and Researchers," *Cisco Systems Website*, 15 July 15 2006 <http://www.cisco.com/en/US/products/hw/switches/ps525/products_case_study09186a0080a3b6c.shtml>.

[5] Aaron Cohen Associates Ltd, & Insight Associates, Inc, "User & Non-user Issues with the Buffalo & Erie County Public Library, *The Buffalo and Erie County Public Library in the Third Millenium*, vol. 3 (Croton-on-Hudson, NY: Aaron Cohen Associates, October 1998) 3. Observations and statistics about non-users are found throughout this volume.

[6] Howard F. McGinn, *ALA (American Library Association), Public Information Office, Campaign for America's Libraries; Academic and Research Library Campaign*, 28 Apr. 2006 <http://www.ala.org/ala/pio/campaign/academicresearch/successfulacademic.htm>.

[7] "Government Performance Results Act of 1993 Home Page," *Office of Management and Budget Website*, 5 May 2006 <http://www.whitehouse.gov/omb/mgmt-gpra/gplaw2m.html>.

[8] Beverly Sheppard, "Perspectives on outcome based evaluation for museums and libraries: Introduction," *Institute of Museums and Library Services Website*, 8 Apr. 2006 <http://www.imls.gov/pdf/pubobe.gif>.

FUNDRAISING

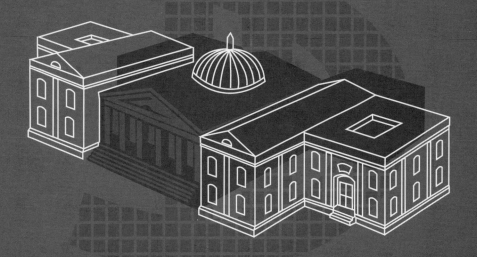

FOCUS ON FUNDRAISING

No matter what constraints or limits bind them, libraries – like all other not-for-profit institutions – base their successful fundraising culture on outstanding service, appropriate marketing and detailed attention to developing, cultivating and soliciting donors.

The most critical and usually least-discussed aspect of successful fundraising is sorting out a group of donors who have motivation, interest and capacity to help the library. Without specific donor prospects in mind, library fundraising will remain unfocused, consuming organizational energy with false starts, and frustrating all who are involved.

Syracuse University is one of the fundraising case studies featured in this book. Speaking at an Academic Library Advancement and Development Network (ALADN) Conference in March 2005, Gregory J. Griffin, senior director of library development and external relations at Syracuse told his attentive audience:

> While development plans vary greatly from library to library, the primary motive for building and maintaining comprehensive development programs are essentially the same: to create an environment conducive to successful fundraising. Successful library development starts with an effective prospect database. Having recently completed the creation of its first comprehensive database of potential donors, Syracuse University Library shares its practical approach to this often-daunting process.[1]

Griffin then lists these questions that help librarians to start thinking about donor prospects:

- Are there existing Library prospect databases?
- Who are the Library's prospects?
- What criteria can we use to identify potential Library prospects?
- How are prospects identified and assigned to development officers at this…institution?
- Who can help us to get the information we need?
- How willing are they to help?
- If we create a prospect database, how should we use it?

While focusing on prospects, consider how donors will be recognized. Establish programs that determine how the institution will keep in touch with donors, letting them know that their gift continues to be appreciated and that the library could accomplish even more with additional contributions. Real library development, whether in a big or small institution, is a professional business that will not be successful without the identification of legitimate prospects and the building of a solid marketing/outreach/donor-recognition culture.

No matter whether your library is academic, public or school, when you consider establishing a prospective donor list, you should consider how to incorporate your user database. Even less affluent schools have found that parents and caregivers of current and recent students often are willing to become donors to the library and/or the program or department where they focused their study. University libraries often find the same dynamic at work among parents of current students. Other donor groups can be developed around subject collections, rare books, special collections, exhibitions and author visits. Public librarians sometimes protest that their user databases are "protected by law." When they consult with library attorneys, however, they nearly always discover that the patron's right to privacy, especially in the use of specific materials, is what is protected by law. As long as that legal right is secure, nothing prohibits public libraries from mining their user databases to find the names of legitimate donor prospects.

Image

A library needs to prepare for and support its fundraising efforts by devising a marketing campaign that positions the institution in the minds of prospective givers. Favorable publicity is especially important if the institution is new to fundraising. Depending on the proposed nature of the campaign, library publicity themes might show how the institution provides services that meet community needs, how it operates in a businesslike way, and how it could provide even more significant benefits to the community if more funding were available.

> No matter what constraints or limits bind them, libraries like all other not-for-profit institutions, base their successful fundraising culture on outstanding service, appropriate marketing and detailed attention to developing, cultivating and soliciting donors.

Even episodic fundraising or small-gift fundraising is most successful when it is accomplished against a background image of success. Regular users, for example, like to be told that the library they are using is striving for success. And, surprisingly for many library professionals, regular users are often willing to become regular donors through annual Friends' memberships, yearly giving programs and tribute opportunities. Libraries must tell their story directly not only to users and potential users but to donors and potential donors. The library message: Your institution is successful in carrying out its mission, innovative in its programming and use of technology, and willing to associate its prestigious community image with the names of for-profit companies, charitable foundations and individual donors who will help it achieve well-conceived and specific plans.

Need

A great deal of library fundraising is both opportunistic and episodic. A college library might seek annual gifts from parents or institutional graduates to purchase a special collection or to underwrite a major exhibit. A public library might seek financial donations to support summer reading or organize a gala to pay for a series of talks by nationally known authors. School libraries might organize a campaign to purchase up-to-date electronic reference databases or to replace worn-out books or book sets.

Breaking out of this episodic model begins when a library recognizes that regular fundraising will help meet critical institutional objectives, such as achieving "the margin of excellence" in the operation of children's outreach services; prolonging the life of rare materials with a paper conservation program; or sustaining the mounting of a quarterly electronic exhibition of library-owned materials on the institution's website. Perhaps small unto themselves, the systematic organization of such events can constitute a strong foundation on which to build a full-scale library development program.

Making Your Case

Most employees can give library management a list of ideas of what they would do with more money. Most fundraising need statements include such listings, but a successful fundraising program is built on much more. It includes a strategic or institutional master plan, overlaid into clear-headed consideration of the cost elements along with a systematic application of library resources – including allocation of administrative or overhead staff costs. Out of this raw material should come a general case statement in which the institution articulates the plan, financial need, time frame, giving opportunities, results for the institution and methods for recognition of the donor for each fundraising project or phase of a capital campaign.

The case statement is both a rationale and an appeal, intended to tap into the basic reasons why people, foundations and governments give money and make grants. In a 1992 seminar, Robert Hartsook, a highly successful university fundraiser, and Suzanne Walters, then director of marketing at Denver Public Library, provided library fundraisers with this list of reasons why donors give.

- Demonstrated spiritual love of humankind gained from spiritual teachings.
- Philanthropic concern for humankind through gifts of time or resources or both.
- Personal gratitude for life or services rendered.
- Perpetuation of personal ideals, values and goals.
- Joining in success to assure organizational goals.
- Fear – prevention of want; assurance of service.[2]

Such lists serve as a reminder that donor prospects bring their own expectations to the table just like the library representatives who are asking for donations. Lists such as this also underscore the need for libraries to translate institutional ideals to relevant, actionable themes and programs. The fact that nearly any ALA survey finds that about two out of three Americans "like," "use," or generally "support" libraries does not automatically translate into financial support. In fact, *Library Journal*, which keeps close tabs on public funding, in its 2006 report demonstrated that voters' willingness to provide new or increasing tax support by raising their taxes had declined steadily over the past decade.[3]

Moreover, when survey questions are shifted from emotional language such as "like," "love" and thinking that "libraries are a good thing" to practical issues such as "how much more personally would you be willing to pay to improve your library (with the list of specific improvements attached), support declines. And, when pressed for answers to "how much more in taxes or tuition or fees would you be willing to pay each year for the next five years to improve your library services," surveyors discover that "support" usually declines precipitously. What these facts indicate is that libraries of all kinds must make *specific* cases for more constituent funding, no matter what the cause or which prospect is being approached. People may "love libraries," but that does not mean they are automatically enthusiastic about giving libraries more money.

Research and Cultivation

Selling libraries is not like selling raffle tickets. It takes more than "cold calls" or periodic flurries of letter writing or a few "galas" or successful book sales to sustain a fundraising program. Unless they are organized as part of a larger context, these efforts only scratch the surface.

In organizing fundraising and researching prospective donors, librarians who are effective fundraisers often find themselves breaking familiar and comfortable patterns of their training and professional life. There is a reason that the word "campaign" is applied to both wartime battles and major fundraising programs. Such development campaigns are about meeting with individuals and groups, dealing with

Libraries must tell their story directly not only to users and potential users but to donors and potential donors. The library message: Your institution is successful in carrying out its mission, innovative in its programming and use of technology, and willing to associate its prestigious community image with the names of for-profit companies, charitable foundations and individual donors.

egos, appointing boards, committees and sub-committees, sorting out prospects, identifying prospects (who may be good friends or library users) by known interest and wealth into categories such as lead gift, major donor, small special project, "no capacity," or "capacity unknown." Meanwhile, other library friends are being organized into other groups, including those who know major donors, those who will talk to or in other ways cultivate which donor, those who will ask for the donations and those who will be "honored" by asking them to join campaign committees and solicitation teams with various degrees of responsibility.

At its simplest, cultivation is getting to know individuals, families, corporate representatives and funding agency officials. At its best, cultivation is a specialized form of courtship that once begun never ends, only ebbing and flowing within the pattern of institutional life.

Funding to Support the Fundraising Effort

To accomplish and sustain this professional level of development activity costs money. In early-stage or episodic fundraising, one or a few regular staff members may handle development activity. If such persons are going to become the library's development team, however, they need training, time (their own, not constantly performing other activities), and support (clerical help, a mailing house, appropriate software and a reasonable expense account are minimal).

University libraries often start and sustain their fundraising with resources provided by their institution's development office. Public libraries and school libraries often have substantial problems when seeking financial support to conduct fundraising. Fundraising efforts can fail, and even at best, they can take several years before the income they generate approaches the annual $10 return in gifts and grants for every $1 invested in costs that stands as a base threshold to measure the success of development offices.

> Libraries of all kinds must make specific cases for more constituent funding, no matter what the cause or which prospect is being approached.

If handled correctly, funds from friends or gifts from private donors do not have the stringent limitations of many publicly-funded revenue streams. If this issue is not handled carefully, bad publicity is just one exposed mistake away.

How to Get Started

There is more – much more – to putting together a successful development program in any library. One way to begin development is to examine successful library fundraising case studies like those presented in this volume. In addition, libraries planning a development program should call on those already experienced in fundraising. Almost every community has individuals working as development officers for organizations such as the United Way or the local or regional community foundation. Usually, such individuals are quite willing to share their knowledge with those moving into the development field.

> In organizing fundraising and researching prospective donors, librarians who are effective fundraisers often find themselves breaking familiar and comfortable patterns of their training and professional life.

In most larger communities, fundraising training is relatively easy to find. Area colleges and universities usually offer short courses on fundraising as part of their extension curricula. Training and contact with area development officers can be found in the programs organized by local chapters of the Association of Fundraising Professionals. *The Chronicle of Philanthropy* (http://philanthropy.com/fundraising/) is the business world's *Wall Street Journal* for fundraisers. Its columns report the news, including large gifts and fundraising companies in trouble, spot trends in giving and receiving, and carry advertisements for training companies and professional fundraising consultancies.

Initiating a fundraising program should also involve visiting successful programs that might offer models or at least good ideas.

Solicitation of Gifts

The most important single point in the development process is the carefully planned solicitation made to donors. No two solicitations are alike. Each solicitation should meet the monetary, emotional and recognition needs of a potential donor. Solicitation is usually done in teams of two and at the most three, with the role of each person carefully scripted. Normally one person undertakes the presentation, with a second serving in a counterpoint and listening role. With two people involved, all the facts and impressions of a presentation and the nuances and details of emotionally charged conversations can be tracked and analyzed.

It is worth keeping in mind a truism of solicitation: The more personal it is, the more effective it is. A personal visit is more effective than a telephone call, which in turn is more effective than a letter. Associates asking known associates, friends asking friends, and high visibility institutional representatives making presentations to a foundation or testifying before a government funding committee constitute the right framework for the personal solicitation process.

In the casebook for their library fundraising seminar, Hartsook and Walters provide a "Checklist of Factors Solicitors Must Consider."[4] They have prepared this list from the donor's perspective. Solicitors who have prepared answers for all of the questions for an individual donor are well prepared to ask for funds. Here are a majority of the points from Hartsook's and Walters' checklist:

> Those starting to plan a development program should call on those already experienced in fundraising.

- Was the solicitation interview thoughtful, well-stated, honest?
- Were the volunteer/staff solicitors well-prepared for determining my/our interests?
- Did they give evidence that they really knew me/us sufficiently?
- Did they get to the point in good time?
- Did they really know the organization, the plan, the [fundraising] program?
- Was the specific request well-stated for a range of giving or merely a yes-or-no figure? Was it reasonable for me/us, given knowledge of my/our background?
- Was the presentation persuasive or matter-of-fact? Were solicitors enthusiastic? Concerned for the urgency of [their institution's] success?
- Is the organization really doing the jobs the solicitors stated? More so? Less so? Was their evidence convincing?
- Am I/are we satisfied/grateful for the organization's services?
- Do I/we really know the organization's leadership, management, staff, volunteers?
- Is the organization well-managed?
- Is the plan for the future reasonable, impressive, persuasive?
- Will our investment make a difference?

- Should I/we provide a modest gift as a test of the organization's efficiency and see how the program progresses, or should I/we provide a real gift of confidence in the organization's plan, leadership, volunteers?
- Is this my/our best investment for our interests, concerns, ideals?
  Is this a way I/we should put back/provide for others as others have provided for us?
- Who else is supporting the organization? What is their record?
  What is the record of governing board participation?
- Did the presenters say what they were giving us?
  [i.e., Does the recognition meet our needs?]
- Why should I/we decide now?

These questions – and others like them – constitute the pattern of expectations that potential donors bring to solicitation meetings. A similar group of questions informs the thinking of members of a funding agency selection committee or a foundation grantmaking board. Library representatives will do well to prepare answers to even the most difficult of these questions before engaging in a solicitation or writing any grant. After every solicitation, especially if unsuccessful, comes analysis. What should happen next? Continuation of cultivation? Another solicitation for a different project? Solicitation for a different level of gift? And so on.

> A truism of solicitation: The more personal it is, the more effective it is.

The fundraising case studies included in this volume show fundraising in a small portion of its infinite varieties.

At Ephrata, PA, Senior High School, Library Media Services Department Supervisor Debra Kachel wrote a successful LSTA grant and trained colleagues to prepare two others. The effort helped fund initiatives to improve literacy in elementary children's writing skills and helped pay for developing a technology curriculum.

At City Academy in inner-city St. Louis, some of the school's board members led in obtaining corporate support, hosting a successful fundraiser, soliciting individual cash donations, and purchasing books for the school from an Amazon.com list.

The stories are shared here with the hope that these examples will guide readers to success in their own project fundraising and in the building of their own institutional development campaigns.

ENDNOTES

[1] Gregory J. Griffin, *Who's Your Donor? A Practical Approach to a Building a Revenue-Producing Library Prospect Database* – Synopsis. Presented at the ALADN Conference, New Orleans, Monday, March 7, 2005. Downloaded on May 4, 2006, from http://libweb.syr.edu/publications/donorsynopsis.doc. Also published in *The Bottom Line: Managing Library Finances*. 18:3 (March 2005), pp. 138-145. The word, "Synopsis," does not appear in the title of the *The Bottom Line* article.

[2] Robert Hartsook, and Walters, Suzanne, *Resource Development for Libraries* Wichita, KS, and Denver, CO: By the authors, 1992, p. 9. Typescript.

[3] Anne Marie Gold. By the People – Library Referenda 2005. *Library Journal*, 131:5 (March 15,2006). Downloaded on May 20, 2006, from http://www.libraryjournal.com/article/CA6314116.html.

[4] Hartsook & Walters, pp. 7-8.

CASE STUDY: SYRACUSE UNIVERSITY, SYRACUSE, NY

"This was the first step in creating a sustained program for library development. This gave us an 'in' to work with every college on campus."

Gregory J. Griffin
Senior Director of Library Development & External Relations
Syracuse University

Challenges

• Library did not have a specific development plan focused on library funding

• No existing model or clear indicator for identifying library donors

• Development officers in most schools and colleges at the University had never included the Library in their funding campaigns

• Unclear how future library programs and expansions would be funded

Solutions

• Hired the Library's first development officer to focus on a library-specific development plan

• Developed a library database of potential donors based on a predictive model of weighted criteria

• Developed a comprehensive development plan based on the predictive model results

• Library's development plan outlines programming for external relations, fundraising, and major giving

Benefits

• The Library has a list of 3,500 likely donors and information about their giving patterns

• Within two years, Library gifts doubled and major gifts increased by more than 100%

• Collaborative efforts with development departments across the University

• Library's development activities are now on par with those throughout the University

• Renewed focus on programming and involvement of local alumni & residents

OVERVIEW

Gregory Griffin was hired in September of 2003, as senior director of library development & external relations. With the appointment, Griffin became the Syracuse University (SU) Library's first officer dedicated to fundraising and development. Not unlike other universities, each school and college within Syracuse had its own development office, focused on fundraising for its respective needs. Along with setting up the Library's development effort, Griffin was asked to work with other SU officials to create collaborative development activities benefiting both the Library and the individual schools.

Working with the University's Advancement Services team, Griffin created the Library's first comprehensive database of potential donors and constructed an effective predictive model to determine levels of interest among potential Library contributors.[1] Using the model, the SU Library was able to review giving patterns and pinpoint likely donors, resulting in a doubling of overall gifts within just two years, and increasing major gifts by over 100 percent. In addition to increased funding, the predictive model led the Library to build stronger relationships with its giving population, influencing library programming, and increasing attendance at events and lectures.

CHALLENGE

With no previous development officer of its own, the Library had relied solely on University funding and occasional unsolicited gifts. Most of the development officers from Syracuse's individual schools and colleges had never included the Library in their fundraising campaigns. As the Library faced expensive challenges ahead, including the need for increased space and state-of-the-art technology, a focused development effort was needed. According to Griffin, "We needed a development plan that we could sustain long term, so we created a very simple, predictive model for the Library to use."

SOLUTIONS

"Our program started with understanding who is already giving to the library. What are the sources and resources that we can look to for help?" reports Griffin. Using SU's database of all university givers, "we did a lot of manual work right up front to gather as many indicators as we possibly could to determine a level of interest in giving to the library," he adds. Griffin's team developed the library's own database of donors following this basic strategy:

1. Review and identify all data fields that can be used as interest indicators for potential Library donors.
2. Review and identify all fields that should be included in a comprehensive database.
3. Populate the database with records that meet at least one of the identified criteria.
4. Create a weighting system to apply to identified criteria.
5. Apply weights to identified records to create a predictive database of library interest.[2]

Griffin's team initially identified 26 criteria as possible predictors of future library donations, including everything from past library donors to Syracuse MLS graduates, people who had worked in the SU Library, and spouses of faculty members. "We had originally thought that people coming up on reunions would be good contributors," says Griffin, but tested against past efforts, such indicators were excluded. From the first list of over 12,400 names, the team weighted each criterion and finished with a core list of 3,498 donor prospects. They closely studied this top group and their past giving records.

"One of the most important things we learned after reviewing the giving patterns of our core list, " he says "was that a large percentage of these donors had given unsolicited gifts to the library as part of their overall giving to the University. Seventy percent of these people were giving to other parts of the school as well."

This revelation of cross-university giving led to a focused campaign to solicit support from development officers across campus. Griffin tapped the Library's specialists and department liaisons to solicit the Library needs from their respective groups, yielding a list of fundable items such as new collections, dedicated space for special programs, and collaborative opportunities. Brochures targeted to development staff were created outlining the shared priorities between the Library and each school. The brochures encouraged schools to include the Library as part of their fundraising campaigns, outlined ways to include the Library as part of their request for donations, and highlighted joint benefits.

Unlike most of SU's other schools and colleges, the model also indicated that more than 30 percent of the Library's contributions had come from non-alumni: parents of students, faculty, and residents throughout central New York. This finding highlighted the Library's support throughout the state and led to a renewed focus on the Library's programming and involvement in the greater community.

The Library's core database list also became a target for increased communications. Each person listed received a letter of introduction soliciting programming input as well as future donations, and was added to the Library's list of newsletter recipients. "The introductory letter alone resulted in donations," beams Griffin, "and began conversations with someone who later gave a $100,000 gift."

Benefits

The Library's development plan, detailing strategies and programs for soliciting new funds, grew from the analysis of the predictive model. The plan's framework outlines next steps in three major areas: external relations programs, fundraising initiatives and programs, and major gift programs. The SU Library now has a clear and confident vision for funding future initiatives.

The benefits of using a predictive model to build a database for the SU Library, and ultimately a focused development plan, are many and the Library staff is optimistic about funding future projects. Suzanne Thorin, SU's dean of libraries, is helping to prioritize large projects, such as building new space for graduate students and developing a multimedia center at the Library.

"This was the first step in creating a sustained program for library development," states Griffin. "This gave us an 'in' to work with every college on campus. Development officers at the other schools like it because we provide them the names and the ideas." Griffin is now recognized as a partner with other development officers and often conducts joint visits to key prospects. As new information comes in regarding major contributors, or as new donors are identified, the data is coded as 'Library donors' and added to the University's database, further positioning the Library as an equal partner with other schools.

With over half of the people identified in the model living within a hundred miles of Syracuse, this information has had a tremendous impact on local Library programming. Offering more lecture series and events, including Banned Books Week activities with the local public library, keeps local SU graduates and supporters involved. By tapping people further who were on the top prospect list, the Library board doubled its size from 16 to 32 members, and the Library's Friends group has grown, increasing their role as Library advocates.

"Students, faculty, and staff are the ultimate beneficiaries of this work," says Griffin. "Our goal is to enhance the resources available to support them. Since developing the predictive model, we've raised $135,000 for a new multipurpose room. It's the Library's largest public space and it now has state-of-the art equipment. We've also raised $100,000 for a music endowment to fund those collections, and we're allocating $200,000 for a library instruction classroom now under construction."

To read Gregory Griffin's paper, *Who's Your Donor? A Practical Approach to Building a Revenue-Producing Library Prospect Database-Synopsis*, which is based on his experience at Syracuse University, visit http://libweb.syr.edu/publications/donorsynopsis.doc.

ENDNOTES

1   Gregory J. Griffin, *Who's Your Donor? A Practical Approach to a Building a Revenue-Producing Library Prospect Database* – Synopsis. Presented at the ALADN Conference, New Orleans, Monday, March 7, 2005. Also published in The Bottom Line: Managing Library Finances. 18:3 (March 2005), pp. 138-145. The word "Synopsis" does not appear in the title of The Bottom Line article.

2   Ibid.

"Our affiliation with a larger library system has provided an economy of scale for subscriptions, interlibrary loan services, circulation, cataloging, and other services that would have otherwise been impossible for Mercantile to handle as a private institution."

John Hoover
Director
St. Louis Mercantile Library

Challenges

- Generate funds to cover annual operating budget

- Make the historic, culturally significant collection more accessible to the widest possible number of users, including students and young people

Solutions

- Join the University of Missouri – St. Louis as a special library

- Move the library to the University's campus, in a new wing attached to the main library

- Join the University's network of funding and services

Benefits

- Affiliation offers an economy of scale for subscriptions, interlibrary loan services, circulation, cataloging, and online resources Mercantile could not have handled as a private institution

- Mercantile gives the University's St. Louis campus its first significant special library collection

- The University of Missouri embraced the Library's original donor base and fundraising efforts

- The University guarantees funds to sustain Mercantile's yearly operating budget

- Since affiliation began in 1996, nearly 10 million dollars in additional operation or endowed funds and trusts have come to the library

Overview

The St. Louis Mercantile Library Association is the oldest general library in continuous existence west of the Mississippi River. At its founding in 1846, the Library was privately funded by the St. Louis Mercantile Library Association, a prosperous and philanthropic group of 19th century merchants. In the subsequent 150 years, membership income and private endowments built an impressive collection recognized by the National Endowment for the Humanities in 1986 for its cultural significance. In 1996, the Library began to reshape its identity for the 21st century, and joined the University of Missouri-St. Louis (UMSL) as a special collections library.

Notably, it moved from the private sector to become part of a public institution, a transfer that also required a change to a different location in the city. Today, the university affiliation enables Mercantile to maintain its full historic identity, providing a level of funding and service support otherwise unavailable, and making the collection available to a wider and younger audience.

For its part, the university campus gained a special library collection with a storied history to enhance its academic programs, and deepen its connection to the region.

Challenge

In 1993, the Mercantile Library directors conducted a critical organizational assessment, and examined its collection, history and mission to gauge the Library's ability to give 21st century audiences the best access to its historic collection. Directors wanted an unvarnished look at the organization's role as a library in an increasingly digital world.

The examination revealed signs of age. The Library was fiscally vulnerable, and located in a low traffic area of the city that isolated the collection from the public. The board's funding scenario for a full operating budget revealed the necessity for increased funding. To generate that sum, the Library would need the equivalent of $25 million in new endowments to yield the investment revenue requisite for annual operation. It was a sum Mercantile could not raise on its own. According to the Library's director, John Hoover, the board then concluded "that future success and a strong identity depended on making the collection more accessible to the widest possible number of users, including students and young people. We wanted to avoid the 'dowager' moniker of a severely entrenched institution with little or no chance of future growth."

Solution

To fulfill the mission to secure wider access, Mercantile turned to the notion of merger as a resolution, and to the University of Missouri - St. Louis, specifically. It is the youngest of the city's campuses, opening in 1966, and the Mercantile board reasoned that the collection would offer the campus an immediate and necessary infusion of regional heritage. In return, the board surmised that UMSL could supply the level of funding and services needed to remain fully operational and to continue building its collections. Hoover recalls that the thought of approaching the university "came as something of an epiphany for the Mercantile board. We knew we were considering something unique. Most small, private libraries like ours focus on maintaining independence and self-sufficiency. They don't think of affiliating with another institution in the manner we were considering."

In 1995, the Mercantile Library board of directors wrote to UMSL inquiring about any interest in a possible affiliation. The university jumped at the chance to welcome its first special library collection to campus, and in 1996 the Mercantile board and the membership of the Mercantile Library voted formally to join UMSL. The final agreement was signed the following year.

The Mercantile Library moved to the campus and into a new, but underused wing attached to the main library. "Of the locations the University offered, we liked the idea of an attached wing, because it would keep us close to the hub of the campus library services and activities," says Hoover. Library staff handled the move themselves, at a cost of $70,000. In retrospect, Hoover recommends that a library considering such a move arrange to retain its original building until six months past the actual move to a new location, to avoid the pressure of having to prepare simultaneously for the removal of an entire collection from the library and for a permanent building closure. "We wouldn't have arranged to sell the original building at the time of the move. The logistics were difficult to manage." Income from the sale benefited the Mercantile endowment.

BENEFITS

Strategic planning with unconventional vision was a key to Mercantile Library's success. The unique approach helped board members pursue a variety of options to push the institution forward. News of the agreement was warmly received. The regional press applauded the move as an opportunity to give the public greater access to historical information relating to the area.

For its part in the agreement, UMSL now boasts a significant special collections library where one did not exist before. The collection and its supporters have strengthened the university's academic programs in the humanities and social sciences, especially history, anthropology and art history; and the library board has served as an active University advisory board for the last decade.

The affiliation agreement embraced the Mercantile Library as a unique and valued addition to the UMSL system. Since 1996, it has perpetuated the historic Library's identity, and embraced the original donor base and fundraising efforts. Guaranteed University funds continue to sustain Mercantile's yearly operating budget. Nearly $10 million in additional operation or endowed funds and trusts have come to the Library in the same period.

"Our affiliation with a larger library system has provided an economy of scale for subscriptions, interlibrary loan services, circulation, cataloging, and other services that would have otherwise been impossible for Mercantile to handle as a private institution. We would not have afforded online resources, for example, without being part of the larger university," remarks Hoover. It has also expedited the collection's growth, opening new avenues to pursue grants, and placed Mercantile's patrimony before the audience it sought after its initial study in 1994.

The Mercantile Library is now the largest special collections library in Missouri and one of the largest in the Midwest.

"Until this crisis, we weren't aware of how the full extent of public support could translate into political and financial action. To gain it, we just needed to be creative, ask, and deliver."

Leslie Rodd
Manager of Grants, Development and Programs
Oakland Public Library

Challenges

- 2003 - a state deficit forced the public library to freeze the book budget and make $1.7 million in budget cuts, including staff and hours of operation

- Identify measures to fund book purchases

Solutions

- Early 2003 - branch librarians posted book wish lists on Amazon.com

- Local bookstores and newspapers joined the Library in a community book donation project

- Late 2003 - The Library rallies local citizens, the Library Friends, and City Council members to support a local tax measure for the 2004 ballot to fund books and keep branches open

Benefits

- Tax Measure Q passes, and the Library increases book collection, and restores hours

- Public support translates into political power

- Library gains higher status among city departments

OVERVIEW

In 2003, California's colossal state budget deficit totaling billions of dollars forced massive trickledown cutbacks in cities and towns throughout the state. In Oakland, the city's $40 million budget deficit forced the public library to freeze the book budget and make $1.7 million in budget cuts, including staff and hours of operation. Faced with massive cuts, library administrators had to determine where to focus efforts to recoup some of the lost funds for essential library services.

Taking a grassroots approach, the Oakland Public Library teamed with local schools, the city council, and a political consultant to rally public support. Efforts took them from posting book donation wish lists online to a successful ballot initiative fourteen months later that boosted the annual budget by over $4 million.

CHALLENGE

Hoping the state's deficit woes would pass, the Oakland Public Library considered short term measures to fund book purchases. By January 2003, as it became apparent that the crisis was entrenched and systemic, the Library considered campaigning for a tax measure to generate needed funds.

The idea conjured a further challenge. By law, any California tax measure requires a two-thirds majority vote to pass. Garnering that voter margin would demand that the Library wage a vigorous public campaign. Library administrators feared that the institution lacked the funding, staffing resources, and expertise for the task.

SOLUTION

In the early stages of the Library's budget cutbacks, Library Director Carmen Martinez and her Administrative Team led the staff focus on local, proactive responses to the situation. "While we couldn't do anything about restoring staff and hours, we believed we could do something about the book budget," says Leslie Rodd, then administrative librarian for program management.

In April 2003, branch librarians turned to Amazon.com and began posting book wish lists. A light, but steady trickle of donations ensued, fed mostly by local patrons. In May, a champion of sorts emerged. Pamela Ribon, author of *Why Girls Are Weird*, discovered the Oakland Public Library's plight and publicized it through her blog Pamie.com. Her first blog about the book budget crisis prompted more than 600 donations. By August, local bookstores and newspapers joined the Library to launch a book donation project called "Oakland Reads." During the summer and through the end of 2003, as thousands of dollars worth of donations flowed to the Library through wish lists, blogs, and the community project, public awareness swelled.

The Library's appreciation for grassroots support grew with each small funding gain. "The success of our unadorned supplication, though certainly not enough to substitute for a healthy stable book budget, gave us more confidence in pursuing a new tax measure," Rodd explains.

As the book fundraising progressed, Carmen Martinez launched a marathon information gathering effort. She attended public meetings, rallies, and budget hearings to learn what Library patrons had to say, speak to those concerns, and voice them to Oakland's elected officials. Martinez was soon joined by the Library Advisory Commission, the Library Friends, and "Save Our Libraries," a group of local citizens formed expressly to respond to the threat of branch library closures, all dedicated to political advocacy on behalf of the Library. "They were most visible at a decisive autumn budget hearing when they packed the gallery with schoolchildren, and spoke eloquently in front of the City Council," remembers Martinez.

Strapped by the deficit, Oakland's City Council was only able to reinstate a small portion of the book budget. Nevertheless, after the dramatic hearing, the Library hired the president of "Save Our Libraries" to help lead a tax campaign measure known as "Measure Q." The stage was set.

Having few resources to retain a professional campaign manager, Martinez and the Library's deputy director Gerry Garzon served as campaign co-chairs, working tirelessly on their own time. In late summer they met with Mayor Jerry Brown and the full city council to discuss a plan to place Measure Q on the March ballot in 2004. Both the mayor and the council supported the measure, and by December, two council members offered to sponsor it.

One of the sponsors, Councilor Jean Quan, suggested the wise tactic of combining the school and library campaigns into one and sharing the costs of running the $150,000 combined campaign. "Oakland is a highly taxed city," Martinez says, "with the property tax bills listing almost a full page of extra taxes. We knew that there would be other tax measures on the upcoming ballot, most notably one for the public schools. Jean suggested we collaborate and bring the two together."

Area resident and noted political consultant Larry Tramutola was hired and lent his professional services to help the Library gauge community interest in the measure. Tramutola and his company, Tramutola Associates, have generated approximately $15 billion through tax measures passed for schools, colleges, libraries, and hospitals. Among his campaign efforts for the Oakland Public Library, Tramutola developed a telephone voter survey about tax tolerance, to give administrators a sense for the tax amount they could request. "We crunched the numbers," recalls Martinez, "to determine the minimum amount we would need to open branch libraries, improve collaborations with schools and increase the book budget to a healthy level."

With only three months to organize and execute, "grassroots" and "sweat equity" became the campaign's operative terms. Martinez and Garzon enlisted volunteers to help put up signs and make phone calls. Employee unions offered up union halls as phone banks, and volunteered for all duties. Local newspapers endorsed the measure through a series of editorials.

In February, one month before the vote, Library administrators organized "Authors Who Care," a fundraising event featuring local poets and authors. A fortuitous anniversary also created an Election Day media opportunity. March 2, 2004, the day Oakland went to the polls, marked the 100th birthday of Theodor Geisel, the beloved author Dr. Seuss. The Library staged a joint birthday party and campaign rally on the steps of City Hall the morning of the election.

Benefit

The people spoke, and Measure Q passed with an astounding 77 percent of the vote, allowing the Library to increase its book collection, restore hours, and begin planning for a future of improvements rather than cuts. By July 2004, branches reopened for Saturday patronage. "After the election, we got right down to work," remembers Garzon. "We were determined to give the public something to show for their money as soon as possible. We wanted them to be aware of our efforts." Almost immediately, the Library ordered small stickers to place on all new books, reading, "Purchased with Measure Q Funds." Each branch celebrated with promotional displays featuring multiple copies of newly acquired popular titles, and Measure Q stickers.

According to Rodd, the successful funding campaign revealed the power of public support to become a political force. "Until this crisis, we weren't aware of how the full extent of public support could translate into political and financial action. To gain it, we just needed to be creative, ask, and deliver," she says. Measure Q's resounding victory also gave the Library a new status among other City Departments, as a more essential service in the eyes of the community than was previously thought.

"We have so much going for us as libraries," Rodd continues. "Working on a community tax measure like this not only forces you to focus on what the library provides the community and what your vision for improved services might be, but it creates solid partnerships that last long after the last vote is counted."

RECOMMENDED READING:

Tramutola, Larry. *Sidewalk Strategies: Seven Winning Steps for Candidates, Causes, and Communities*. TurnKey Press, November 2003.

"Collectively, all of the board members have a strong sense of personal responsibility to see the school programs succeed. One member takes the lead on an idea, and soon after a different member will propose another quality idea. We talk about their preferences and goals and work to create an opportunity to fulfill their goals while at the same time meeting the goals of the Library."

Ginger Imster
Director of Development
City Academy

Challenges

• Expand the school library's book collection without budget funding

• Raise funds and secure book donations from local businesses and individuals

Solutions

• Board of directors initiates community outreach for school library fundraising, including:

– Area bank encourages book and fund donations at summer concert series

– Asset management company selects the library as recipient of employee holiday giving fund

– Development Committee member hosts annual cocktail "For the Love of Reading" reception fundraiser

Benefits

• $121,947 total cash and in-kind contributions donated to the City Academy library in the 2005-2006 school year

• Library book collection swells from 75 to 7,000 in three years

• Successful board member initiatives inspire quality responses and ideas from other members

OVERVIEW

Founded in 1999, City Academy is a private, independent, scholarship-based elementary school, offering instruction to students from junior kindergarten through sixth grade. The Academy's school library has grown from a collection of about 75 books to a collection of 7,000 in three years, overcoming significant funding challenges in the process. Donor support from throughout the St. Louis area sustains the Academy's emphasis on scholarship and financial aid, but covers only a very small portion of the Library's operating budget. Guided by the efforts of an active board of directors, the Academy employed unique and highly effective grassroots techniques to transform the Library from a new space starving for a collection, to a bustling focal point supporting the school's reading-centered curriculum.

CHALLENGES

City Academy's annual budget subsidizes the school's emphasis on scholarship. Forty percent of the budget is funded by investment income from the school's endowment. Twenty percent of the Academy's total annual revenue is from tuition and fees. The remaining 40 percent comes from the broader community. With funding spread thinly, the Library receives only a modest budgetary allocation. In 2002, that fact was clearly evident in the tiny collection of 75 books in the large library space. Expanding the collection required funds generated outside the budget, and administrative staff brought the urgent need to City Academy's board of directors. "We are a reading-centered program, and everything we do focuses on reading, but we have a small fundraising office, so we rely on volunteers to help with special events and projects," explained Director of Development Ginger Imster.

SOLUTION

Involving the board was a wise choice, given its proactive commitment to the school and historical ties to the community. All members of the City Academy board of directors are personally dedicated to the school's development and act on behalf of the school as advocates in the community. "Collectively, all of the board members have a strong sense of community and involvement," says Imster. "They possess a high level of loyalty and have a strong sense of personal responsibility to see the school programs succeed." A look at the board reveals the following:

- One-third – long-term board members with strong ties to the community and dedicated to education
- One-third – contemporaries of school co-founder and president Don Danforth - natives of St. Louis who once tutored children at the Mathews Dickey Boys' & Girls' Club, the local organization from which City Academy grew; Age: 30s and 40s.
- One-third – newer members recruited since the Academy's opening, friends and associates of the first two groups of board members

"Their dedication encourages peer-to-peer initiatives," explains Imster. "One member takes the lead on an idea, and soon after a different member will propose a quality idea. We talk about their preferences and goals and work to create an opportunity to fulfill their goals while at the same time meeting the goals of the Library." Four examples of City Academy's successful fundraising programs are described below.

FINANCIAL INSTITUTION REACHES OUT

A board member employed as a vice president at UMB Bank jump-started the library book collection drive in 2002. He convinced the bank's public relations department to contact the school and propose a book drive during the company-sponsored summer concert series. Working with the bank's public relations contact, Imster and City Academy Assistant Director of Development Nikki Doughty set up areas for book and fund donations at the concert pavilion, and arranged to speak briefly to audiences about the school and its needs.

The bank also installed drop boxes at its branches, and added information about City Academy to all customer receipts, spreading the word among the larger community. "It was a wonderful way to approach the broader community for support of our program and the library specifically," said Imster.

CORPORATE HOLIDAY GIVING

Another board member employed at the Asset Consulting Group (ACG), which specializes in high net worth management, suggested book donations as an objective for the company's December employee holiday giving drive. Participating ACG employees could either donate books, funds, or purchase books from a published Library wish list.

City Academy Librarian and Reading Specialist Martha Brown worked with another library specialist to develop the book title wish list with input from faculty. It requested that donors purchase books through Amazon.com and arrange for direct shipping to the Library. The Library staff followed up on the effort by reserving a day when donors could tour the Library and read with students, giving donors an opportunity to experience the impact of their fundraising efforts.

COCKTAIL BOOK PARTY FUNDRAISER

A Development Committee member volunteered to host a cocktail event at her home to benefit the City Academy Library in February 2006. Invitees attending the first annual "For the Love of Reading" reception had the opportunity to purchase remaining books from the wish list, and learn more about the school and its needs from Imster, Doughty, Danforth, Brown, and invited parents. "We thought it would be easier to buy the books ahead of time," Imster recalls, "and then have them on display at the event so guests could pick the books they wanted to buy and donate them to the school immediately."

The invitee list numbered 750, and the planners hoped for a 10 percent acceptance return as an indication of success. The goal was met with a final tally of 75 guests.

Event Logistics: The event required one month of planning, but Imster suggests a window of two months.

Hostess and Development Committee member Barbara Landesman secured and paid for the evening's catering needs. Imster, Doughty and colleagues created and mailed invitations, accepted RSVPs and advance book purchases. "We worked together to generate the guest list from among the sponsor's friends, community volunteers, donors and Academy parents. And because we were able to work with vendors to defer the payment of the books until after the event, most of the expenditures were simply time," remarked Doughty.

Invitation Materials: Heavy duty card stock
Color printer
Plain, white greeting card envelopes
Access to computer e-mail
Postage ($293)

Using both standard and electronic mail for invitations yielded some unexpected results. "We got a really nice response from the invitation that went out via e-mail," notes Doughty. "We attracted some new donors who had not been familiar with the school in the past."

THE POWER OF ONE

A new member of the City Academy board of directors adopted the library as a personal "pet" project. She approached a number of friends and family for donations to underwrite the cost of new books for the library. Her appeal generated both cash and book donations.

BENEFITS

In three years, the City Academy library book collection has mushroomed from 75 books in 1999 to 7,000. The students now have a bona fide collection to support their reading needs. The Academy board plans to hone its effectiveness with additional training and materials available through the Independent Schools Association of the Central States, and the National Association of Independent Schools, www.nais.org.

$7,947 – Total Cash Donations to the City Academy in 2005-2006

$12,500 – Since 2004 the UMB bank has donated this amount in unrestricted funds used to underwrite a portion of the school's Scholarship Program. The bank initiative described for this story generated countless book donations from 2002-2006.

$1,062 – The ACG employee holiday giving campaign raised $1,062 in funds and book donations. The Library sent the company an update on its programs at the end of the 2005-2006 school year. Imster plans to ask the board member who assisted with the event to repeat their efforts in December 2006.

$3,155 net revenue – Planning the cocktail party fundraiser, Imster and her colleagues set a goal of $2,500, to recoup the cost of book purchases and make a small fundraising profit.

The combined guest list of donors and Academy parents proved fruitful, as the parents' presence proved compelling. "It meant a lot to the donors to meet some of the parents," says Imster. "They were terrific ambassadors and advocates of the school; it was really powerful to have them present that night." In the end, the event earned a gross of $5,055, twice the goal, or a net of $3,155, and introduced new people to City Academy's unique program.

Imster and Doughty tracked purchases carefully, and personalized each book with the donor's name and a personal inscription. Among the titles guests purchased were vital reference materials, the Coretta Scott King Book Award Collection, and a Shakespeare Library. Reception thank you notes were printed on note cards featuring student art work.

The cocktail party fundraiser will continue as an annual February event to benefit the Academy.

$1,330 – the new board member raised the amount after soliciting library donations from friends and family.

$500 – a single restricted gift specifically for the Library made by the Library's major volunteer.

Total In-Kind Donations:

$105,000 Total In-kind value of donated books
$8,000 Total In-Kind value of volunteer time (annual)
$1,000 Donated catering services (Love of Reading Reception)

Figure 1.
Excerpt from the City Academy
"beacon" Newsletter; Winter 2006

CASE STUDY: EPHRATA AREA SCHOOLS, EPHRATA, PA

"A successful grant not only generates money, but also good publicity and exposure for a library and its programs. The key is to write application materials from your school's unique perspective, in the language of the grant. Don't make a reviewer search for your ideas."

Debra Kachel
Supervisor of Library Media Services
Ephrata Sr. High School

Challenges

• Secure grant funds to support information literacy and curriculum goals

• Offer technology solutions to support students and curriculum

Solutions

• Experienced grant writer submits a winning grant application

• Grant writing workshop to instruct and guide district librarians with the application process

Benefits

• Much needed funds to support necessary school and library initiatives

• A core group of district librarians has acquired necessary skills to research, apply for, and secure grant monies

• Publicity and recognition for the library and its programs

OVERVIEW

Department Supervisor of Library Media Services Debra Kachel submitted successful grant applications and her efforts earned the Ephrata public school libraries three Library Services and Technology (LSTA) grants, totaling $135,000. The awards served close to 3,900 children in five elementary schools, a middle school, and a high school. The district applied the funds to a state initiative to improve literacy and writing skills among elementary school students, and also created a much needed technology curriculum. As a seasoned expert on grants, Kachel conducted workshops to teach the district librarians grant writing skills, and they in turn wrote successful grants.

CHALLENGE

The Ephrata public school libraries needed grant funds for two significant programs: to participate in a state initiative to improve information literacy and writing skills among elementary school students, and to create a school technology curriculum. Also needed was expertise – skilled grant writers with the experience to gather information from contributors, state Ephrata's monetary need, and communicate with precision the planned objectives and merits of grant applications.

SOLUTION

Debra Kachel has enjoyed success writing education grants in her work as program director and adjunct instructor for Mansfield University's online school library and technologies graduate school, where she teaches grant writing in a course about school library advocacy. For the Ephrata Area School District, Kachel wrote and secured the first LSTA grant request for funding in support of the purchase of laptop computers for the high school.

Eager to share her knowledge and build a core group of qualified grant writers for the school district, she organized workshops for the Ephrata librarians who would pursue LSTA grants for the following year. Using her successful grant application as a model, Kachel and the librarians selected the next school library applicant from their district. They worked with teachers at the targeted school to develop the grant idea, selecting the area of need that was most urgent, and most applicable to the grant parameters.

Kachel then gave the librarian group a primer on grants and grant writing. She shared examples of winning applications, focusing on the lexicon of grant guidelines and the need to mirror that language in any application. She also reviewed the element of requesting school letters of support, offering the following pointers: request letters that highlight the school's unique perspective, its experience, its challenges and designs for the grant.

After the initial instruction, work shifted to the group's specific grant application. Members split into subgroups responsible for different sections of the grant, thus breaking the task into manageable pieces. Drafts went to Kachel for review and suggestions, and the final pieces formed one application.

With her guidance, Ephrata librarians applied for and garnered the two subsequent LSTA grants for district elementary schools. In all, the libraries earned a total of $135,000 with the LSTA grants for the high school and two elementary schools. The three grants funded the purchase of 25 laptops per school to be used to teach information literacy, and development of a technology curriculum.

DEB KACHEL'S GUIDELINES FOR SUCCESS

Is there a secret for success? Yes, according to Kachel – perspective, patience, and practice. "The key is to write from your organization's unique perspective, in the language of the grant. Don't make a reviewer search for your ideas." As with the Ephrata librarians, Kachel offers the following tips:

- Apply to be a grant reader. It gives you an opportunity to read grants and see what works and what does not. Contact your state's school library advisor and volunteer.
- Read grant guidelines carefully before starting the application process.
- Don't keep reviewers searching: use the exact language of the grant, and don't hide the information they are looking for. Be concrete and specific.
- When writing a letter of support, write from your organization's perspective.

Kachel often refers to the following resources:

Browning, Beverly A. *Grant Writing for Educators*. Bloomington, IN: Solution Tree, 2004.

Hall-Ellis, Sylvia D., and Ann Jerabek. *Project Design*. Grants for School Libraries. Westport, CT: Libraries Unlimited, 2003.

Benefits

The guidance of an experienced grant writer such as Kachel secured a number of benefits:

- Technology resources for students in area schools
- Professional development for school librarians
- A core group of people with specialized knowledge to research grant funding opportunities for the school district
- Recognition for the library and its initiative

According to Debra Kachel, "A successful grant not only generates money, but also good publicity and exposure for a library and its programs." In Ephrata's case, it also breeds success. Armed with their new knowledge, the Ephrata Area School District librarians worked together as a team to draft another successful application that, in early 2006, secured a district-wide collection development grant in which each of its seven libraries will receive $5,000 for new print science resources. More evidence to show that the district schools, the students, and her peers have gained much from the grant initiative – including valuable resources, expert advice, and skills for the future.

[1] "Fund Raising." (www.philanthropy.com/fundraising). *The Chronicle of Philanthropy.*

Though not library specific, this is an excellent source of current fundraising practice.

[2] *Knowledge to Build On.* (http://foundationcenter.org). The Foundation Center.

The Foundation Center's mission is to advance knowledge of US philanthropy for non profits and its website has both specific information on funders as well as information about fundraising techniques.

[3] Burnett, Ken. *The Zen of Fundraising: 89 Timeless Ideas to Strengthen and Develop Your Donor Relationships.* (San Francisco: Jossey-Bass, 2006)

Burnett gives practical and successful techniques for building fundraising relationships from his experience as a professional fundraiser.

[4] Hartsook, Robert. *Closing That Gift: How to be Successful 99% of the Time.* (Englewood Cliffs, NJ: Prentice-Hall, 2005)

This book presents practical fundraising ideas that work from an expert and philanthropy consultant.

[5] Swan, James. *Fundraising for Libraries: 25 Proven Ways to Get More Money for your Library.* (New York: Neal-Schuman, 2002)

Swan presents an overview of fundraising techniques that will help librarians select the best way for their library to obtain needed funds.

GETTING STARTED

Here are a few steps to take that will make your efforts more effective:

1. Identify a list of projects that need funds. Describe several projects and create an information sheet on each that describes the project, why it is important and how much it will cost. If raising money for general library support, describe how the funds raised will be used and specifically how monies raised will improve the library.

_____

_____

_____

_____

_____

_____

2. Identify possible donors. Who can you contact to raise money for the specific projects you have identified, or for the library in general? Is there a list of past donors? Can you ask donors to your school, university or city to give specifically to the library? Can you trade or buy lists of donors to other nonprofit organizations?

_____

_____

_____

_____

_____

_____

3. Plan how you will approach donors. Set goals, a timeline and identify methods of communication (letter, phone, speech, grant application, personal call, etc.) you can use.

_____

_____

_____

_____

_____

_____

4. Identify or recruit people to carry out fundraising. Which library users, staff or board members can help identify donors? Are there community, school or university leaders who can help you raise funds?

_____

_____

_____

_____

_____

_____

5. Keep track of your contacts and their donations. Plan how you will thank donors and publicize the results of the campaign as a whole. What accounting will you set up for donated funds? How will you ensure that donated funds will be spent in a timely manner on appropriate expenditures? What kind of database will you use to track and manage your donor list?

_____

_____

_____

_____

_____

_____

6. Analyze both successes and failures. What techniques worked and why? What didn't work? What should you modify in the future?

_____

_____

_____

_____

_____

_____

Technology and eResource Management

Clearing the Technology Fog

Former Librarian of Congress Daniel J. Boorstin captured the principal issue in technology-induced change in libraries when he remarked, "Technology is so much fun but we can drown in our technology. The fog of information can drive out knowledge."[1]

The first dangerous icebergs in Boorstin's "information fog" involve the complexities in the choices to be made, both vertically and horizontally. Vertically, this is demonstrated with each library purchase. An electronic catalog system, for example, offers unlimited choices through customization, with each modification incurring an additional cost and end user impact. The horizontal complexity is exemplified by the breadth of technology options required to efficiently operate a modern-day library. These include decisions about:

- Infrastructure: network, security, firewalls, bandwidth, routers, telecommunications, voice mail and interactive voice response (IVR), etc.
- Hardware: servers, databases, computer terminals, printers, copiers, RFID or other electronic tags, scanners, cameras, wireless phones or PDAs, fax machines, telecommunications hardware, etc.
- Software: server applications, web applications, database applications, computer OS and work tools such as Microsoft Office and Adobe Acrobat, integration of software and databases via XML or web services, database linking, link resolvers, web portals, Really Simple Syndication (RSS), PDA and handheld applications, patron information management, billing and order management, financial applications, etc.
- Design and architecture: the look and feel and navigation usability for web portals and software, design and management of application integration, design of technology architecture, special considerations for the location of technology to best serve library users.
- Vendor options: which vendors to do what, vendor ability and willingness to cooperate with each other and library staff, whether to outsource or attempt to control technology options in-house, etc.

The second group of icebergs in the technology fog relates to costs. Regardless of whether they serve universities, schools or communities, libraries operate with limited resources. Operating within these finite limits, libraries pushed to improve technology-based services, frequently cutting spending in other areas to make electronic installations. Hence, the new computers and database access subscriptions arrive at the cost of books, or fewer children's programs and/or cutbacks in outreach to constituents, whether they are faculty, business professionals or children. This challenging financial reality is the primary reason why grants play such an important role in library technology innovation. The Bill and Melinda Gates Foundation grants, for example, have paid for Internet-connected computers in thousands of public libraries.

What most new technology innovators fail to realize is that purchasing new library hardware or software is only the tip of a cost iceberg, the depth of which usually cannot be seen when the innovation process begins. This hidden cost accumulation starts with an installation cost that customizes the technology innovation to a particular library's facilities and IT environment. That cost is followed by others: maintenance, regular backups, training of staff and users, debugging after crashes, downloading and uploading software upgrades. Furthermore, as technology and software popularity increases, more staff hours are required to watch over more machines and more programs, and to provide customization that streamlines the operations of often-used search routines at the institutional, building or machine level.

The least anticipated cost is that of time. Staff members or contract training specialists require extraordinary amounts of time to train staff to proficiency or expert status and to instruct users in hardware maintenance and search routines that allow them to use the growing number of computers in the library, their homes or offices. Moreover, staff must manage and provide appropriate one-on-one help on in-library computers and, select appropriate software packages and databases that will meet user needs. When a librarian has the appropriate training, library customers receive the kind of optimal help that Neal Kaske, director of statistics and surveys, U.S. National Commission on Libraries and Information Science (NCLIS), describes in the tagline of his e-mail signature plate. The tagline reads, "An hour on the Internet can often save you five minutes at a library reference desk." That's the level of service most users hope for, and expect, when they visit their university, public or school libraries. To save a user's time, library staff time always is involved in one way or another.

NEW LIBRARY SERVICE OPTIONS

Although technology changes library cost factors, it also adds service options. And that's why so many librarians have moved to adopt technology options so quickly. The case studies in this book reflect that adaptation.

At Millersville University in Millersville, PA, Coordinator of Access Services Professor Scott Anderson led a team of students in development of a software package to manage the library's resource database and to customize its look and feel. The new "Axis Admin Tool," as it is called, allows subject librarians to locate all information on a subject with a single search, post customized descriptions of databases for any subject or course, add a resource to multiple website areas at one time, and update descriptions and resource links from a single access point. The SQL-based software results in enriched access to resources such as EBSCO's *Academic Search Premier*. The innovation saves time for librarians, faculty and student users.

Albert Riess, reference services and electronic database librarian at the E. H. Butler Library at Buffalo State College in Buffalo, NY, followed a similar path, bundling all EBSCO databases into two megadatabases, simplifying searching for students. Now they can point and click online and differentiate scholarly articles from other offerings.

Lesley University Libraries in Cambridge, MA, innovated to improve library service to its off-campus users who constitute 50 percent of its student body. At the Library's request, EBSCO Publishing developed a password program so that students could access the company's databases. Library staff then borrowed the open-source Searchpath tutorial from Western Michigan University to create an interactive learning program that students could access so their searches would be faster and more fruitful.

GUIDELINES FOR SUCCESSFUL TECHNOLOGY INNOVATION

In their March 22, 2006 presentation at the Computers in Libraries Conference, Gwinnett County Public Library staff members Michael Casey, Branch Manager, and Chris Hall, IT Coordinator, recommended that librarians consider the following factors in making good technology decisions:

Mission and Goals
Under their first heading, *strategic planning*, Casey and Hall remind librarians that "If technology serves no goal then it serves no purpose. Technology plans and decisions need to be true to an institution's mission, as reflected in its service goals and strategic plan."[2]

Understand Organizational Culture

Library technology decision makers need to understand your library's culture, particularly its technology culture. That knowledge includes recognizing if your library is "Bleeding Edge vs. Leading Edge vs. Close Follower" in the timing and method of its new technology adoptions. Next, how does your library make its technology leaps? Does the library "buy it off the rack?" Do you build it yourself? Or do you "piece it together from existing parts?" Next, the authors review the role of IT staff within the culture: "Do they play a part in all levels of planning and decision making?" "Are they brought in early or only after the idea has been decided upon?" Or, worse, "Are they only brought in after the product has been purchased?" Finally they ask librarians to analyze their organizational attitude about vendors: Does the organization like to use a "single vendor" or "best of breed?"

Emerging Technology Team

Casey and Hall recommend establishment of an "Emerging Technology Team" as "an outward looking group." The members of this group function as lookouts who scan and rescan the environment to match emerging technology options with their library's service needs. What the authors are advocating is the creation of an internal change team, a group of staff who watch changes in technology on behalf of their work specialties. The advantage of this team is that it creates a receptive climate where new technology ideas get a fair hearing before the organization's change resisters start finding fault with the options.

Stay within Budget and Building Limits

The authors' recommendations on budget and buildings are straightforward: Live within the organization's budget and remember that "community needs" take priority over technology regarding the use of facility space. Casey and Hall might well have added that identifying and articulating "community needs" is one of the most difficult jobs that professional librarians have, no matter the nature of the institution. Their overall budget advice is pertinent, however. Library managers need to carefully evaluate the hard costs, soft costs and the benefits of all their technology choices before they make any actual investment.

> Live within the organization's budget and remember that "community needs" take priority over technology regarding the use of facility space.

Cater to Constituents

Casey and Hall use "return on investment (ROI)," as an assessment category for how to weigh the potential impact of technological innovation. Moving away from economics to social surveys, they suggest that libraries need to consider how technology will impact customer service, staff efficiency and circulation, along with real and virtual library visits. To make these assessments, the two library practitioners might have added the importance of formal communications with current and potential users about how they regard a proposed set of technology changes. Formal conversations via focus groups, public hearings, listening sessions with specific groups of users, and structured enumerations using telephone interviews add clarity to every library decision.

The purpose of all such meetings is the same: To ensure that the end user is the number one focus in all technology design and purchase decisions, and, as closely as possible, to match up end user expectations with the possibilities. In the end, this catering to constituents by focusing on individual users is the best filter to use when making all technology purchase and design decisions. Will one standard platform work better than five more specialized platforms? Is training appropriate? Do end users want to link to electronic full text or browse well-organized shelves of paper copies? Are end users accessing library products from home over land lines, remotely via wireless connections, or only when they visit the library? Is the website or portal design consistent and user friendly? Is performance equal to user expectation? What is the best combination of technology, software and access pathways to maximize their positive experiences?

Cautionary Advice

Casey and Hall conclude with two pieces of good advice: "Set your expectations before implementation and stick to them during the [innovation] review" and "Be willing to change or discard anything that's not giving you what you need," because "It's easier to change *now* than later!"

> Libraries need to consider how technology will impact customer service, staff efficiency and circulation, along with real and virtual library visits.

Consider Larger Questions

Finally, as we innovate technologically, we need to recognize that computers and high speed communication are redefining the way we work and socialize with each other. In the library profession, new technology is transforming the service environment, redefining the most basic services and forcing the re-asking of important questions like "What is a great library?" and "What is quality library service?" Who, a decade ago for example, would have envisioned the need to integrate virtual and place-oriented services as a requirement for defining the quality of a library's operations?

It is difficult to keep such important philosophical questions in mind when we recognize that inevitably and inexorably "information technology" just keeps changing. This passing parade of options can be illustrated by the simple task of listing the dates of Public Library Association *Tech Notes*, which are "short, Web-based papers introducing specific technologies for public librarians." These notes are selected for publication by the members of the PLA Technology Committee and written by library technology guru Dick Boss.

Though directed specifically to public librarians, *Tech Notes*, with their original and revision dates, are a wonderful mirror of what a conscientious group of professional library leaders, ranging from directors and IT specialists to operations officers and various services managers, select as the issues that need introductory or explanatory notes. The topical list follows, with the month (when known) and year each topic was written and or rewritten.

A glance at the list shows that no one type of technology topic dominates: Instead the subjects include communication devices (RFID, WiFi), policy issues (statistics and CIPA), attempts to summarize economic and financial subjects (e-business, dealing with vendors), and new librarian organization schemes (metadata, Unicode and GIS).

The list mirrors the nature of library technology change: Trying to adopt innovations that show promise, staying within budgets, and dealing with the social regulation of technology while keeping old customers happy and winning new ones. These tensions can be seen in the PLA Technology Committee's willingness to commission *Tech Notes* on RFID and WiFi, even as the new hot topics on the library technology shelf, Blogs and Wikis, are postponed as so simple or so marginal as to not capture the committee's attention at that moment.

PLA Tech Note Topics, 1999-2006

2006	Date of Origin	Date of Revision
Wireless LANs	4/04	3/06
Voice Over IP (VOIP)	3/06	
Libraries and RSS (Really Simple Syndication)	3/06	
RFID Technology	3/01	2/06
2005		
Mobile Computer Devices in Libraries	5/05	
Digital Content Management	5/05	
Library Web Portals	1?/02	Rev 5/05
2004		
Virtual Reference	3/01	Rev 12/04
Web Services 12/04		
Open URL	12/04	
Remote Conferencing	4/00	Rev 12/04
E-Commerce: A Muddled Picture	12/04	
Electronic Resource Management	4/04	
Filtering Technology & CIPA Compliance	9/01	Rev 4/04
E-Books	6/00	Rev 4/04
2003		
Network Management	12/03	
Negotiating Contracts with Database Vendors	10/03	
Unicode: From Chinese to Cherokee; from Kana to Klingon	6/00	Rev 10/03
Software for Children	5/03	
Geographic Information Systems (GIS): Mapping the Territory	5/00	Rev 10/03
2002		
Automated Storage/Retrieval and Return/Sorting Systems	6/02	
Disaster Planning for Computers and Networks.	4/00	Rev 4/02
Client Server Technology.	2/02	
2001		
Metadata: Always More Than You Think	4/00	Rev 5/01
2000		
Push Technology: Pushed to the Brink.	4/00	
Rethinking Library Statistics in a Changing Environment	4/00	
Digital Object Identifier (DOI): The Persistence of Memory	4/00	
Intranets: The Web Inside	4/00	

Dealing with information technology and the opportunities for technology innovation have an emotional cost on the library profession. Noted e-library columnist Michael Stephens, who has institutional affiliations with St. Joseph County Public Library (South Bend, IN) and the University of North Texas School of Library and Information Science (Denton, TX), captured this issue in a 2004 *Library Journal* article. He writes that libraries have to see their individual users as "technology consumers [who] have evolving expectations of what the library should provide. Yet new technologies can be disruptive to both staff and public. Added to all this, some of us [i.e. library professionals] remain technophobes while others are consumed by technolust—an irrational love for new technology combined with unrealistic expectations for the solutions it brings."[3]

Within this complex environment, the case studies in this chapter relate how individual libraries have managed and used technology in ways that have captured the attention of their users and of other librarians as well. Their stories follow.

ENDNOTES

[1] Barbara Gamarekian, "Working Profile: Daniel J. Boorstin; Helping the Library of Congress with its Mission," *The New York Times* 8 July 1983.

[2] Michael Casey and Chris Hall, "New Technology Challenges & Successes," *Computers in Libraries* 2006, 21 Aug. 2006 <http://www.infotoday.com/cil2006/presentations/D103_Casey_Hall.pps>.

[3] Michael Stephens, "Technoplans vs. Technolust," *Library Journal* 129, no. 18 (2004): 36-37, *Academic Search Premier*, EBSCO*host*, 21 Aug. 2006.

"I had an idea to bundle our databases into two mega databases. The search experience would be simplified for users, and still retrieve scholarly research results. Students could improve their online research skills without sacrificing the Internet experience they're used to.

EBSCO's technical assistance is a big reason why the idea became reality, and the database project hit the ground running."

Albert F. Riess
Reference Services & Electronic Database Librarian
E.H. Butler Library, Buffalo State College

Challenges

- Improve student academic online research skills beyond commercial Internet search engines

- Help students identify scholarly and peer reviewed article sources

- Combine college's range of EBSCO*host* databases into two streamlined mega databases

- Help students quickly access the online full-text of "real" articles from magazines, newspapers, & journals

Solutions

- Collaborated with EBSCO Publishing Technical Support team to create "ArticlesOnline FAST" and "Peer Reviewed Articles EZ"

- Introduced new customization at summer workshop for reference librarians

- Publicized new databases with:

  – Reference desk handouts

  – 2'x3' posters in Library's computer workstation area (2 styles)

  – Campus E-mail, Campus Newspaper

  – Student Information Sessions

Benefits

- Reference Librarians actively use databases in library instruction; faculty reaction positive

- Students like databases, especially for ease of use

- Databases offer a simple point and click online experience, and retrieve scholarly research results

- Database usage has increased by 23%

- Students improve their online research skills without sacrificing the Internet experience they're used to

Overview

Buffalo State College Reference Librarian Albert Riess created two mega online databases, by bundling and customizing several EBSCO*host* products to give students both full text online periodicals, and scholarly research data in a simple search environment. Launched for the 2005 fall semester, ArticlesOnline*FAST* and Peer Reviewed Articles *EZ* are meeting student and faculty requests for a strong library research platform with the speed and simplicity of a commercial Internet search engine.

Challenge

In the spring of 2005, Riess and other colleagues at the E.H. Butler Library were fielding requests to build student academic research skills beyond the use of commercial Internet search engines. Too many students were using Internet search engines to retrieve what they thought were "articles," while professors were requiring students to use magazine, journal, or newspaper articles for class reports. A large number of course assignments required scholarly and peer-reviewed references, and many students could neither identify nor distinguish peer-reviewed journals from other journal types.

After resolving a number of inquiries, Riess concluded that the Library might be able to customize some of its resources to help students lay a stronger research foundation without sacrificing the speed and simplicity they were accustomed to using the Internet. "Thinking about the problem, I remembered that the Library's EBSCO Publishing databases allow simultaneous searches across multiple databases, and offer many customizable features for administrators," says Riess. "It seemed logical to me that there must be a way to use the EBSCO*admin* profile to bundle databases and search features together into two mega-databases. Both would retrieve information with streamlined, uncomplicated search criteria, giving students a comfortable search environment. Information retrieval would literally be just a couple of clicks away." He envisioned one full text database with only full text articles, and another specializing exclusively in peer-reviewed content.

Solution

Riess solicited the help of Alison Galati, Customer Relations Manager at EBSCO Publishing, and together they worked behind the scenes in EBSCO*admin* to navigate, test, and customize the database and search features. They tested adjustments for specific groups of databases, and various limiters and settings, such as full text and publication name, to see what would best meet the project's needs. For example, applying the full text limiter in Riess's project made sense, as he wanted to restrict results to only full text. "Al drove the process from the beginning," notes Galati. "We set up a series of phone trainings, and reviewed all of the EBSCO*admin* settings. We discussed the pros and cons of each scenario extensively, and tested each possibility in a painstaking and deliberate manner. As a result, Al fully understood what would work and what wouldn't, and why, each step of the way."

After three months of testing and customization, Riess realized his vision. The bundling process eliminated the need for users to select EBSCO databases, yielding a pared down Advanced Search screen that automatically retrieved results with the limiters and features Riess assigned using EBSCO*admin* (See Figure 1.).

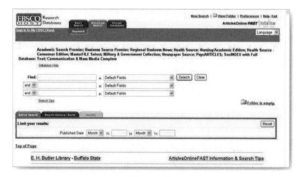

Figure 1.
ArticlesOnline *FAST* search screen

ArticlesOnline*FAST* and Peer Reviewed Articles *EZ* became the new "mega" databases. ArticlesOnline*FAST* gives students quick retrieval of full text articles across many subject areas. Peer Reviewed Articles *EZ* presents citations and full text articles from standard peer reviewed journals.

Riess launched the databases at the beginning of the 2005 fall semester, following a successful training workshop for the reference librarians. The E.H. Butler Library website, http://www.buffalostate.edu/library/, was redesigned to prominently feature direct links to the new databases to promote easy access. "We wanted the information to be right up front, visible, and one click away for students," says Riess. (See Figure 2.) Other important publicity included posters and handouts with database information and search tips, displayed at the reference desk and the Library's computer workstation area (See Figure 3.).

Figure 2.
Buffalo State E.H. Butler Library website,
http://www.buffalostate.edu/library/

Campus communication included e-mails to faculty and staff, and advertisements in the student newspaper. Riess and other reference librarians promoted the databases to students themselves, setting up information tables with posters in both the student union and the library lobby area. A journalism student even wrote and published an article about the database project for course work.

BENEFITS

Reference librarians are involved, the faculty reaction is positive, and students are catching on. "Once students come to us," says Riess, "we're able to make a difference. I've asked students for their honest impressions about using the databases, and the responses are very positive." Faculty report that Peer Reviewed Articles *EZ* is a valuable resource when they need peer reviewed articles that cross disciplines. The reference librarians have openly embraced the new database configuration, introducing it in library instruction classes as an important starting point for collegiate research.

Riess is pleased that users are responding to the simpler point and click experience of the Library's online databases and retrieving the scholarly research results they require for academic success. Usage statistics support this trend. By the end of the fall 2005 semester, there were nearly 58,000 searches conducted in the two databases, an increase of 23 percent over the previous year. "That's what I had hoped for," says Riess. "EBSCO's invaluable technical assistance is a big reason why the databases hit the ground running, and we've never looked back."

Figure 3.
Posters Displayed at
Reference Desk and
computer work stations

CASE STUDY: THE MISSOURI RESEARCH AND EDUCATION NETWORK (MORENET), COLUMBIA, MO

"Our members are growing, and facing more complicated issues: handling large amounts of data, running curriculum tools and conducting multipoint video conferences. The ability to have a fast and reliable Internet connection is crucial to conducting business today."

Marsha Goldberg
Product Support Representative
MOREnet

Challenges

- Need to provide vendors with improved tools to upload IP addresses

- Provide network monitoring and usage data tools to consortium members in a secure environment

Solutions

- MyMOREnet Internet portal

- IP delivery tool for vendors

- Reporting functionality for consortium members

Benefits

- Easy to use Internet-based tools for vendors and consortium members

- Reliable Internet technology means tools are available 24/7

- High level of customer satisfaction with MOREnet services

OVERVIEW

The Missouri Research and Education Network (MOREnet) provides Internet connectivity, technical support, videoconferencing services and training to Missouri's K-12 schools, colleges and universities, public libraries, health care, state government and other affiliated organizations. MOREnet was established in 1991, and operates as a unit within the University of Missouri.

MOREnet is committed to providing value-added services that increase member satisfaction and meet user needs. When surveyed by a private research firm, MOREnet members rated their level of satisfaction at 9.1 out of 10. Additionally, MOREnet's primary service – providing reliable Internet connectivity for Missouri public schools, higher education institutions and libraries –earned a near-perfect rating of 9.5 out of 10.

That commitment sparked a period of careful research in 2004, during which time the large consortium explored improvements to its network monitoring tools. The fruit of that study is MyMOREnet, a technology solution that allows MOREnet's diverse membership to analyze their network activity in a secure computing environment, and to better manage their relationships with the organization's technical support staff.

CHALLENGE

According to Product Support Representative Marsha Goldberg, MOREnet's front line technical support team delivers high-level support for Internet connectivity, from backbone services and network support, to desktop support. "MOREnet is unique because of the scope of our membership—who we serve and how we serve them," she says. Members range in size from libraries operating two days per week with a part-time staff, to very large institutions. "Our members include primary and secondary schools, universities, hospitals, and non-profits. We provide technical support on all levels for all customers. Most statewide consortia only cover a part of what we do," Goldberg adds.

As a result, MOREnet has a high volume of member and vendor demands for interactivity and data. MOREnet's Internet Protocol addresses (IPs) are constantly changing, due to the consortium's constant growth and members' changing needs. "IP range tables are both long and complicated, and accuracy in the transmission is critical, so that all of our member organizations are able to take advantage of services such as IP authentication to EBSCO*host*," says Goldberg.

In recent years, providing access to large amounts of important member information in a secure computing environment proved problematic. Confidential IP information and related data could be viewed on web pages with unrestricted access. Data upload tools were cumbersome. MOREnet's IP delivery system for vendors was difficult to use, and unreliable.

SOLUTION

In 2003, MOREnet introduced MyMOREnet to consortium members. The web-based interface gave authorized administrators quick and secure access to on-demand utilization reports relating to their data connections. Designed by MOREnet's programmers, MyMOREnet offers an intuitive interface that users can navigate with little or no training. Additional plug-ins have been added to the interface since its inception, allowing members to submit technical requests online, and to use additional security and utilization tools for managing data connections. The additions also afford administrators the ability to assign different levels of access permissions to others in their organizations.

In 2004, Goldberg researched solutions by which consortium vendors might retrieve IP information quickly and conveniently. "We needed to make information available simply and securely. It was clear that previous solutions were outdated and cumbersome," Goldberg remembers.

The results of her research led to the creation of a MyMOREnet access feature for vendors. When vendors need to obtain the latest set of MOREnet IPs, they log into the MyMOREnet secure site. Only the applications and utilities specific to the accessing vendor are displayed. Once logged in, a vendor can view IP changes and IP ranges in HTML or comma-delimited formats.

In addition to IP access, MyMOREnet offers vendors the ability to subscribe to weekly e-mail alerts notifying them of IP changes. Vendors are excited about the new features, as they represent a vast improvement in IP delivery. It's also easy for MOREnet to investigate any discrepancies. The tool allows MOREnet staff to call up and search an entire set of IPs all at once.

Consortium members also enjoy the benefits of MyMOREnet functionality. Members can log into My-MOREnet and run network utilization reports, including bandwidth usage reports generated on the fly. "Our members are growing, and facing more complicated issues," Goldberg remarks. "The ability to have a fast and reliable Internet connection is crucial to conducting business today. Our members are handling large amounts of data, running curriculum tools, and conducting multipoint video conferences. Many larger customers use MyMOREnet reports and functionality in tandem with their own network utilization utilities," she says.

Most recently, MOREnet released a network monitoring tool called Palantir, which allows members to view networking reports, determine current outages or router problems, run pings and traceroutes from their routers, and designate an e-mail address to receive outage alerts. Plans to deliver more and more services to members via the MyMOREnet portal are in development.

BENEFITS

The MyMOREnet Internet portal makes it easier for consortium members to track the health of their Internet connections. "It gives our members more complete information, and choices as to what's going on with their networks," says Megan Gill, MOREnet's marketing and communications manager.

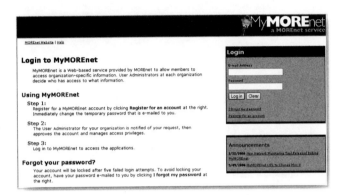

Figure 1.
MyMOREnet

It also grants them a degree of freedom. Members and vendors can access the interface 24 hours per day, and seven days per week. If desired, they can submit technical support request "tickets" electronically, for such needs as DNS changes, without having to make a phone call to technical staff during business hours. EBSCO Publishing Customer Account Specialist Holly Sullivan speaks to the benefit of using MyMOREnet as a vendor. "MyMOREnet really helps us to provide better service to EBSCO Publishing customers across Missouri. I have new IPs automatically e-mailed to me each week. I don't have to remember to log in and check for them. It's very efficient and easy-to-use."

As Goldberg notes, the consortium's technology solution is also a boon to the technical support staff. "In the whole scope of support," she concludes, "MyMOREnet is a good application, easy to use, and low maintenance. It was a great idea to create a new system rather than maintain a legacy system that didn't work well."

Examples of MyMOREnet used with permission from MOREnet, http://www.more.net/.

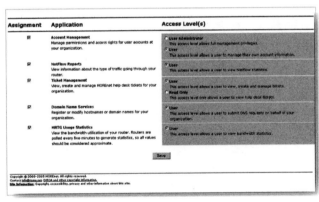

Figure 2.
MyMOREnet

CASE STUDY: LESLEY UNIVERSITY, CAMBRIDGE, MA

"We need to create the best Web environment for student research with Lesley's online library resources. We are their resource. The more smoothly things operate for staff and students, with less library intervention, the better it is for us."

Constance Vrattos
Associate Director
Lesley University Libraries

Challenges

• Needed a Web environment for information literacy instruction. 50% of the student population is off campus, without access to a physical Lesley library

• Needed a quick and effective student login process to enable student practice searching in a "live" EBSCO database tutorial

• Create a tutorial that is interactive, easy, specific, and interesting, to promote successful student research

Solutions

• Created Searchpath tutorial to help Lesley student population in diverse environments learn about and access library resources without the need for authentication

• Lesley software solution: open-source Searchpath tutorial from Western Michigan University; with PHP and Flash

• EBSCO Publishing developed a password system consisting of the first five digits of a student's identification card to enable "live" database searching within the tutorial

Benefits

• Lesley students across the country learn to access, evaluate, and use information for their research

• New students have ease of access to practice database searching in EBSCO

• Lesley University Library on interaction with students - "We are their resource. The more smoothly things operate for them, with less library intervention, the better it is for us."

• View Searchpath at http://www.lesley.edu/library/searchpath

OVERVIEW

To accommodate the library needs of a substantial distant learning student population that represents 50 percent of its enrollment, Lesley University Libraries developed Searchpath, an online tutorial environment where students can learn information literacy concepts, practice database searching, and access research services by remote library access. Essential for the solution's effectiveness is the tutorial's password login process created by EBSCO Publishing, which allows users to search databases from within the tutorial modules. Searchpath debuted in 2004 and has enabled more than 800 Lesley students nationwide to build a strong foundation in library research, in both undergraduate and graduate fields of study.

CHALLENGE

Lesley University, located in Cambridge, Massachusetts, is unique in terms of its academic programs and student needs. Fifty percent of the student population, graduate and undergraduate, learns off campus at remote sites through distance education, including independent study and/or online learning across 23 U.S. states, and around the globe. These students have no physical access to a Lesley library building, yet require the same access to specialized subject research services as their on-campus peers. "We are their resource," states Constance Vrattos, the Libraries' associate director. "We need to create the best Web environment for student research with Lesley's online library resources."

Creating the environment posed two challenges. First, the tutorial vehicle for teaching students how to use the Libraries' online resources would have to be effective and interesting enough to hold the user's attention; in short, it had to be fun. Second, the solution would also require easy access for on-campus and distance students alike. Web access to library e-resources via referring URL at the actual library building would need modification to accommodate off-campus use. For that, Vrattos and Holmes turned to EBSCO Publishing's Customer Support Team for advice and assistance.

SOLUTION

An analysis of the challenges during the 2003-2004 academic year yielded Searchpath, an interactive and comprehensive series of engaging, online tutorial modules that create an environment within which students can learn information literacy concepts and practice database searching within Lesley's library system. (See Figure 1.) The tutorial was funded by an information literacy grant from the Massachusetts Board of Library Commissioners (MBLC), and models open source software developed by Western Michigan University, also called Searchpath, and the University of Texas TILT Tutorial.

Lesley revised the content and design of their own modules with PHP open-source web page programming and original illustrations to better match the needs of its graduate degree students in education and human services.

With Searchpath, students learn to access, evaluate and use information appropriate for their research. A central feature is the opportunity to practice searching in a live EBSCO database, with all accessible features. The tutorial features six self-paced instruction

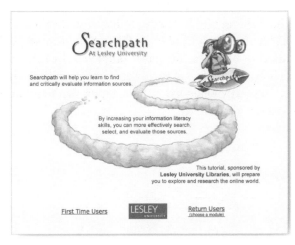

Figure 1.
http://mail.lesley.edu:81/searchpath/

modules covering academic information sources, narrowing a topic, choosing keywords for searching, finding articles and assessing online materials. Other modules review searching the Web and avoiding plagiarism. Each module includes text and interactive activities, followed by a brief quiz. The quiz results may be e-mailed to the instructor for accountability.

The fourth module, Finding Articles, features EBSCO's *Academic Search Premier* database, with coaching to help students perform a keyword search, view full-text articles, and assess the results. The EBSCO Publishing Customer Support Team developed a Search-path password login for Lesley, consisting of the first five digits of a student's identification card. (See Figure 2.) This gives students quick and effective entrance into the live version of *Academic Search Premier* within the tutorial, bypassing the library's referring URL link to EBSCO's electronic databases, which might otherwise restrict or prevent access. (See Figure 3.)

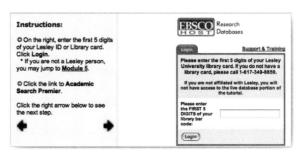

Figure 2.
http://mail.lesley.edu:81/searchpath/mod4/
11-database.php (use 11152)

The EBSCO password solution does not check an Internet protocol, or the previous web page a user visits before attempting a login. Instead, it incorporates login rules into a separate URL, forcing users to enter the site by means of the five-digit code only. "EBSCO Publishing is the first vendor we think of for online partnerships," concludes Vrattos. "Customer Satisfaction is always more than ready to help us find creative and effective solutions for our staff and students. The more smoothly things operate for them, with less library intervention, the better it is for us," concludes Vrattos.

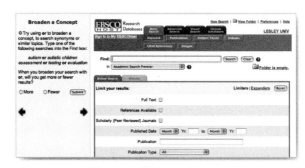

Figure 3.
http://mail.lesley.edu:81/searchpath/mod4/
11-database.php

Since the program's debut in September of 2004, over 800 students have completed the Lesley Searchpath tutorial and built a quality foundation for their library research. Students based in Alaska, California, Colorado, Georgia, Idaho, Maine, Massachusetts, Nevada, New Mexico, Ohio, Oregon, South Carolina, and Washington state have completed the tutorial as part of their Masters in Education program with Lesley. Reaching out to its constituents with technology solutions, the Lesley University Libraries have successfully extended online resources and a thorough, well-conceived vehicle of resource instruction to a national audience.

CASE STUDY: MILLERSVILLE UNIVERSITY, MILLERSVILLE, PA

"By customizing Library resource descriptions, and promoting resources in new ways in different academic areas, subject librarians can leverage their work to other faculty members. The tool we developed has allowed us to manage our web presence and leverage what's been done."

Scott Anderson
Professor, and Coordinator of Access Services
Ganser Library
Millersville University

Challenges

• Help library faculty assign online resources to multiple areas of academic study on the Library website

• Find an alternative to DOS computing environment

• Create an online tool that allows Library faculty to write and share customized descriptions of resources in order to promote Library resources to university students and professors.

Solutions

• Library Faculty and student software developers created the Axis Admin Tool, which allows university librarians to:

– Locate all existing information about a resource on the Library website, in one search

– Post customized descriptions of the databases relating to a given subject or course listing

– Assign a database to multiple subjects and course listings

– Easily add a resource to multiple areas of the Library website

– Update descriptions and links for a resource from a single access point

Benefits

• The Admin Tool maximizes the value of the Library's existing electronic and database resources by making them available and accessible to professors and students across fields of study

• The tool leverages the use of resource descriptions and link maintenance

Overview

The Ganser Library at Millersville University created the Axis Admin Tool to broaden university access to database information. The tool makes it possible for library faculty to analyze and annotate electronic documents and databases and then post these under multiple subject and class listings. Thus, it maximizes the value of the library's existing electronic and database resources by making them available to professors and students in their particular fields of study. The software also speeds link maintenance and resource distribution and saves staff time in the process.

Challenge

In 1996, the Ganser Library was using a very basic DOS-like software environment to list web-based library resources under appropriate academic subject headings. Library faculty found this environment too restrictive, however, because it forced them to choose only one academic subject area for each resource. A resource that might be well suited to three different academic areas could fall under only one. As a result, valuable database information was isolated from the university population, and from relevant instructional activities.

The Library faculty, including Professor Scott Anderson, the coordinator of access services, set out to develop alternatives that would allow them to assign library resources to multiple categories with descriptions appropriate to various subjects and courses already established on the website. "In the process, it would maximize the value of the Library's existing electronic and database resources by making them available and accessible to professors and students across fields of study," Anderson explains, "while leveraging the use of resource descriptions and link maintenance."

Solution

Working with Millersville students who acted as software developers, Anderson created what became the Axis Admin Tool, using Microsoft SQL, ColdFusion middleware, and a Visual Basic application. The Admin Tool, as it has come to be known, operates as a library management tool to maintain the Library website database and some aspects of the site's look and feel. A listing of all Library resources and their descriptions are stored in the tool's SQL database. "We went with SQL to hold everything, because Microsoft Access didn't meet our needs," says Anderson.

Maximizing the Visibility of Resources on the Library Website

The Admin Tool delivers five important functions unavailable in the former DOS environment. Using a template of features tab, it allows subject librarians to:

- Locate all existing information about a resource on the website in one search.
- Post customized descriptions of databases as they relate to specific subjects or course listings.
- Assign a library database to multiple subjects and course listings with one input.
- Easily add a resource to multiple areas of the library website.
- Update e-resource descriptions and links from a single access point.

Anderson explains, "Imagine that the communication subject specialist has a resource database link, such as *Academic Search Premier,* with a suitable web description. The business specialist might want the same link, but prefer a different database description more suited to business courses. With this tool, the business librarian can write an additional description and list it with the database under a course heading."

Figure 1: Axis Admin Tool Showing Database Name and Department Listings

Figure 1 shows the EBSCO database *Academic Search Premier*, and a general description. Subject librarians can write additional descriptions such as those seen in Figure 1: math, film studies, literature, music, and geography.

The tool also allows librarians to borrow, but not edit, existing descriptions they did not create and to use them in their own postings. If an author edits one of his or her own descriptions, the changes display instantly across the library's website, affecting every occurrence of that particular database description.

Figure 2: Information on a Category Tree

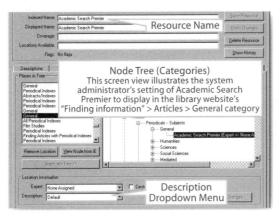

Moving on from descriptions, Library faculty members scroll through a site category "node" tree to add resources or descriptions to one or more subjects or course guides. Unwanted descriptions can be deleted at the same time.

For example, EBSCO Publishing's *Academic Search Premier* database is posted to more than 200 locations throughout the library website, and the node tree feature enables library faculty to alter its position on the site, all 200 if desired, from one single, central administration point, saving valuable time.

"By customizing online resource descriptions, and promoting resources in new ways in different academic areas, subject librarians can leverage their work to other faculty members. The tool we developed has allowed us to manage our web presence and leverage what's been done," says Anderson.

BENEFIT

The Axis Admin Tool affords a 50 percent time savings to the University's library faculty, compared to the original DOS-like menu system. The time savings eases workloads. Anderson relates, "When our consortium changed vendor contracts, it took me only 30 minutes to change product links within our admin database, and I was done." Without the database driven website, every instance of that link would have had to be identified and changed, consuming considerably more time and energy, since the links were not centrally managed. The faster update time also improves Anderson's ability to serve users of the Library website by improving or eliminating messages specific to particular resources.

The Admin Tool also promotes Library faculty collaboration. "The tool has allowed us to manage our web presence and leverage what's been done. By customizing resource descriptions, and promoting resources in new ways in different academic areas, subject librarians can leverage their work to other faculty members," says Anderson.

An additional benefit of this university initiative comes in the technical training of Millersville undergraduates who have helped create, maintain, and upgrade the tool. The students gain experience developing specifications and functions as they work to make each version better than the last.

To view examples of listings that result from the Admin Tool, go to the Library's website at www.library.millersville.edu. Follow site navigation to Library WebSite > Finding Information > Resource Guides.

Ganser Library Director David Zabatsky is happy with the tool's functionality and results. Usage of Library resources typically exceeds that of similarly sized universities, and the word is spreading to other Pennsylvania State System and Keystone Library Network Libraries. Scott Anderson has made several presentations to the Keystone Library Network during consortial conferences in Pennsylvania. California University of Pennsylvania is now using the software in a production environment, and Bloomsburg University of Pennsylvania is testing the software as well.

Plans for enhancement are also in the works. Customized, end user-driven elements are slated for addition to the software. Anderson is incorporating functionality similar to MyLibrary[1] to give students access to library resources relating specifically to their majors. "Students will log into MyLibrary, and library resources and services relating to their majors will be pushed out to them upon login. It will then allow them to shape their research environment and tailor it to their specific study needs," he says.

For libraries interested in pursuing a similar solution, Anderson emphasizes that "developers have to be familiar with database structure and SQL, some web presentation functionality, and in our case, some Visual Basic technology." These are increasingly common skills but identifying staff in sufficient number to develop a similar tool can be challenging.

ENDNOTES

[1] MyLibrary was developed by Eric Lease at North Carolina State University. A related *Library Journal* article about this: www.libraryjournal.com/index.asp?layout=article&articleid=CA323338.

CASE STUDY: PHOENIX PUBLIC LIBRARY, PHOENIX, AZ

"Every content owner is a Library intranet technology decision maker. They helped determine how this tool would perform, and the technology allows them to maintain the data they need to perform their work."

Alvaro Meythaler
IT Project Manager
Phoenix Public Library

Challenges

- Find a technology solution to help staff keep pace with updates to internal library documentation

- Give staff greater access to library information through the use of technology

- Free up webmaster from responsibility of content updates

Solutions

- Staff Source intranet functions as the Library's main communication tool

- Staff Source gives staff a central information access point for bibliographic and collection management services, library administration, information technology, and patron services

- Online intranet forms enable staff to become content owners (i.e. calendar of events)

- Built from open source software, reducing Library costs

Benefits

- Staff Source allows staff to update and manage content on the intranet and some areas of the public website

- Staff Source generates more efficient and faster staff responses to customer inquiries

- Webmaster no longer involved in event calendar updates; focuses exclusively on bona fide IT issues

- Staff Source is accepted as an essential source for library documentation

OVERVIEW

In 2004, the Phoenix Public Library developed a third generation intranet to meet the growing demands for staff's easy access to information infrastructure and the ability to update and maintain guidelines, procedures, and other essential library data. Known as Staff Source, the intranet was built with open source software, and functions as the library's main communication tool for content and data management.

According to Alvaro Meythaler, the Library's IT project manager, Staff Source is also the fruit of a staff-centered approach that draws heavily on feedback from each Library work unit. "Acquiring a better internal information delivery and maintenance tool was the Library's mission," he says. It was a far-reaching mission. Meythaler is responsible for IT operations and support, enterprise systems, ILS management, and web development services that support the Library system's 15 branches, 600+ employees, and approximately 12 million items in annual circulation. "Staff Source is our main communication tool," Meythaler concludes. "With it, all library system employees stay informed and up to date on standard procedures."

CHALLENGE

The Phoenix Library staff struggled to keep pace with updates to internal Library documentation, including manuals and the events calendar. Maintaining currency in the hard copy archive of Library manuals and calendars was difficult, and reprinting hard copies of each updated version proved expensive.

Furthermore, most staff members lacked access to Library event information, aside from printed copies posted in various building locations. Requests for calendar edits or additions filtered through Jesse Haro, the Library's webmaster, because only he had internal access to modify or update the electronic version of the calendar data. As a result, the work of calendar data input began to detract from Haro's more pressing responsibilities as webmaster.

To address these issues, the IT team invited all Library supervisors to gather for brainstorming sessions to discuss their goals for an intranet repository. They discussed features and content they wanted to help complete tasks efficiently, and formulated training objectives for staff. Together, they developed essential criteria for a technological solution that would provide updated information to staff with improved internal documentation and communication among all work units.

SOLUTION

After several months of research, development and testing, IT deployed Staff Source, an intranet customized to the content management needs of the staff. The solution reflects the creativity and vision of the webmaster Jesse Haro, and gives staff a central information access point for bibliographic and collection management services, library administration, information technology, and patron services. (See Figure 1.)

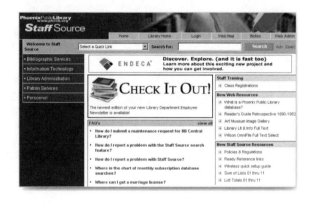

Figure 1.

For example, the ability to view staff manuals, to update internal Library information, and better communicate that information to employees, emerged as essential requests from staff surveys. Staff Source functionality centers on the staff's ability to easily view and update content. In fact, the system's content is managed wholly by the staff. Each staff unit responsible for a system wide activity designates its own intranet content owner to add, edit, or delete specific information in the intranet system. Usually, a supervisor takes this role. The list of content owners is posted on Staff Source, and all employees know to go there for contact information.

To facilitate the staff user experience, the Library developers decided to retain the existing native file formats for all content. Meythaler explains, saying, "After our initial survey and brainstorming sessions, it was decided to use web-based content management, and retain the documentation formats we already used, such as Word, PowerPoint, Excel, and PDF. This would help us maximize what we already had, and help make the intranet user-friendly." The native formats are well suited for a closed computing environment like an intranet, readily downloadable, and printer friendly.

Employees have individual Staff Source accounts, and can customize their view of the Library's intranet information by bookmarking internal links, in their individual accounts, be it a collection management spreadsheet, the monthly newsletter, a new library policy, or a report on the latest usage data for a constituent population. Staff can also bookmark external links like search engines, book vendors or their preferred reference websites. This allows them to access to their bookmarks from any computer in the system.

Another area in which the Library pursued ease of use and improved communication was the online events calendar. To remove the Library's webmaster from sole responsibility for continual updates to calendar content, Jesse Haro created an online events form for users. The learning curve wasn't steep; calendar webmaster training for new supervisors requires less than thirty minutes.

Once a proposed event is approved, a staff member opens Staff Source and uses radio buttons to select the relevant subject area and branch. From there, essential information is entered in a simple form, including name, start and end dates, and how often the event will occur. The event then immediately populates the online calendar, allowing staff and the public to view it on the public website. Haro also created e-mail forms for the calendar on the public site, which enable library customers to set e-mail event reminders to themselves and family members, as seen below. This feature makes communication about the calendar more convenient, and gives library customers a role in publicizing local library events. (See Figure 2.)

Figure 2.
http://www.phoenixpubliclibrary.org/events.jsp

Marketing an Intranet Technology Solution

The Library promotes the use of its intranet through visibility, current technology, and ease of use. Staff Source is set as the default home page for all Library staff computers, and an easily navigable site map guides users to the intranet categories they need.

Updates to the system are highly visible; new links appear in their related content areas and on the main page. RSS technology also features prominently, giving staff the ability to see new documentation added to Staff Source.

An annual online survey solicits feedback about Staff Source, and asks respondents to rate their system. The system immediately tabulates the survey, allowing department supervisors to review results, note areas of success, and make any needed recommendations for improvement.

The Technology behind Staff Source

The IT staff reduced costs by designing Staff Source entirely from open source software.

- The application server - from the Apache Software Foundation http://jakarta.apache.org/tomcat/index.html
- The database server (RDBMS) - from http://www.postresql.org
- The operating system - from Linux Online, http://www.linux.org
- The JSP Scripting Language (Java) - from http://java.sun.com

Would Meythaler recommend this solution to other libraries? "I would definitely recommend the creation of a Staff Source intranet as a communication tool for employees," he says. However, libraries should be aware of the pros and cons associated with open source technology. Small libraries may not have the technical expertise to develop a similar tool. And, because this customized intranet is built in situ, "libraries must possess developers' specific and detailed documentation in order to maintain the system, especially if the specialist moves from the library," Meythaler stresses. He recommends that libraries needing sustained technical assistance might be better advised to invest in corporate software and product-specific customer support.

BENEFITS

Staff Source is fully established in the Phoenix Public Library culture. The staff refers to it as their source for essential library documentation.

The technology that sustains Staff Source has softened the boundaries between library divisions and work units. "Every content owner is a Library intranet technology decision maker. They helped determine how this tool would perform, and the technology allows them to maintain the data they need to perform their work," explains Meythaler. Short, formal training sessions are available to new employees, but the forms are designed simply enough to learn by clicking and browsing.

This process frees IT staff from the cumbersome task of content maintenance. Specialized IT staff members become involved with Staff Source only when there are bona fide IT issues, such as broken links, or design changes to the site.

The public benefits are equally rewarding. The Library's intranet solution generates more efficient and faster staff responses to customer inquiries. When a customer submits a question or offers feedback on the public website, the information goes to a database displayed on Staff Source. A librarian can then consult the answer on Staff Source, from a detailed and categorized list of internal FAQs and suggested responses, and then respond. If an answer is not available, they can create a response and later add the answer to Staff Source for future use.

Other public libraries have also contacted Meythaler to express their interest in the Staff Source concept, and to seek recommendations on how the Phoenix model might be incorporated for their librarians.

Alvaro Meythaler expresses the overall benefit in simple terms. "Staff Source succeeds as an intranet because everyone uses it. Everyone recognizes it as the gateway that leads to essential library information."

[1] *Pew Internet & American Life* (www.pewinternet.org) and *Pew Society and the Internet* (www.pewtrust). Pew Charitable Trust.

These two research-based websites deal with leading edge technologies and use and impact of the Internet on society.

[2] *TechAtlas Technology Planning Tool* (www.webjunction.org). Web Junction.

This online product will help librarians assess current hardware, staff skills and technology needs. Web Junction also has articles discussing every aspect of technology in libraries.

[3] Burke, John. *The Neal-Schuman Library Technology Companion, Second Edition.* (New York: Neal-Schuman, 2006)

Burke covers all aspects of technology in libraries with an emphasis on managing electronic resources in all types of libraries.

[4] Campbell, Nicole. *Usability Assessment of Library-Related Websites: Methods and Case Studies.* (Chicago: ALA/LITA, 1998)

Though an older copyright, this book will help librarians sort out how patrons use online resources provided by the library. This provides both public library and academic examples.

[5] Pace, Andrew. *The Ultimate Digital Library: Where the New Information Players Meet* (Chicago: ALA, 2003)

This book focuses on work with vendors and how to keep up with the fast rate of change that surrounds information technology.

GETTING STARTED

Managing all forms of technology in libraries is an ongoing process. The following are steps to help staff to change or improve technology services.

1. Define a specific technology project. Identify what technology is required (website, in-house computers, staff intranet etc.) What is the desired result of the project in terms of improved service? Who is the target audience? Does hardware or software need to be changed or be upgraded?

_____

_____

_____

_____

_____

_____

2. Determine who needs to be involved in the project. Identify specific staff members including technology staff, public service staff, purchasing, consultants, etc. Do staff skills match what is needed to complete the project successfully? What training will staff need? Does staff have the time to include work on this project? Who will lead this project?

_____

_____

_____

_____

_____

_____

3. Anticipate disruptions to staff work or public service that may occur during this technology project. How can you minimize disruptions?

_____

_____

_____

_____

_____

4. Prepare a communication plan. How will you communicate progress on this project to staff and the public?

_____

_____

_____

_____

_____

_____

5. Create a timeline for work and intermediate goals by which you can measure progress. Develop a budget for the project.

_____

_____

_____

_____

_____

_____

6. How will you know you have been successful in meeting your goals? How will you measure increased use of this technology? How will you know the impact of this use on staff, customers or the community?

_____

_____

_____

_____

_____

_____

LIBRARY MARKETING

Change Marketing, Marketing Change

Libraries need to market to match changing realities.

Marketing has to adapt to appeal to a changing population: Gross increases or decreases, shifts in ages, income and education, and migrations to different companies, colleges and communities mean that the service population of libraries always is changing. Moreover, tastes and needs shift, as when a majority of mothers with young children enter the workforce; customers expect higher levels of personalized service; and people of all ages want the ability to serve themselves quickly and conveniently.

Or, technology alters the way individuals and families approach markets of all kinds including libraries. Such shifts are observed when parents and children alike expect to use the Internet to "go to the library in their pajamas" from home; others expect drive-through libraries; and technologically adept users expect staff of even the smallest libraries to know as much about electronic databases and searching as they do. These shifts occur in a communications climate where an increasing percentage of the population obtains its news and its advertisements electronically rather than from print sources.

This new emphasis on marketing and outreach also reflects the reality that campus, public and school libraries aren't the only games in town anymore. Dr. Christine Koontz, director of the Florida State University GeoLib Program, writes that it is the:

> element of competition that is turning library users into customers. Like it or not folks, we no longer have "patrons" who graciously accept what the library profession selects and offers. The new library user demands, chooses, and selects among information products. And that means that the "patron" of old is really a customer! So, if library users are now customers, what should we know about the characteristics of customers?[1]

This new emphasis on marketing and outreach also reflects the reality that campus, public and school libraries aren't the only game in town anymore.

Elements of a Marketing Program

The answer to Koontz's question is found in the theory of market segmentation. Koontz defines market segmentation as

> subdividing a market into distinct subsets of users that behave in the same way or have similar needs. Segments for the library could be demographic (Asian); geographic (branch-level); psychographics (leisure-oriented); customer size (largest user group area); benefits (have children in the home learning to read.)[2]

In the simplest terms, "market segmentation" means that library marketing programs need to be addressed to specific individuals within various marketing segments. When we have identified those segments, we can plan and evaluate the success of our marketing to those segments. No individual wants to be thought of as "everybody." Market segmentation respects individual and group differences. When a library understands the marketing segments it serves, it can plan and execute specific marketing programs that appeal to these groups.

With target markets identified, libraries then consider using another classic marketing tool, a review of the "4 Ps." Adapted to libraries, these are:

- **Product** – involves the library service offered and how much trouble and cost is involved in providing it. A persistent danger in libraries is trying to offer too many products and services without allocating enough resources to make them outstanding. Effective marketing begins with creating the right high-quality product or service. To put this issue another way, just like other successful businesses, libraries need to be market-driven rather than supply-driven. When library customers expect Internet-connected computers, it does little good to offer them manual typewriters. When library constituents of all ages are moving wholesale to MP3 players or iPod®s, we can expect audiotape, CD and DVD collections to receive less, or at least different use, regardless of advertising. Offering the right product to the right constituency is as basic to library success as it is to any private business.

- **Price of Service** – in the private sector is the cost that consumers pay to use a service or buy a product. Libraries need to consider this factor by asking "What does using a particular library service cost the library user?" Their "costs" include customer time, mode of transportation or communication to "pick up" the product or use the service and the "inconvenience" of other activities that can't be done when using the library. Busy commuters on the way home, for example, will drive only a few blocks out of their way to pick up a reserved book. People put a high value on the time it takes them to acquire a book. Waiting in line to check out materials, having to look through "too many books" to find a new best seller, reserve and reference-questioning wait times, a library website that seems hard to navigate and the "trouble" of getting or renewing a library card all are implicit costs that raise the "price" of using a library.

- **Place** – considers the delivery and distribution of products and services, including transaction location, availability, and accessibility. After spending only a short time in any working library, staff recognize the power of place in all library use. The most powerful place in most individual life is "home." The second most powerful place is "at work." The growing power of the Internet is changing the definition of both. In considering all of the factors in the first line of this paragraph, it is wise to ask "At what place should our library offer this service or product?" Individuals and groups define "place" very differently, and cheaper technology, more expensive paper publishing costs, rising fuel prices, and the adoption of the Internet as a personal and business communications form will dramatically affect the meaning of place in North American libraries through the next decade.

- **Promotion** – concerns how libraries let users know what products are available. Library professionals need to consider all possibilities in laying out a marketing promotion. A neighborhood billboard or transit-cards will be more effective with potential library users than advertising in a newspaper. A radio public service announcement will catch a different clientele than a bookmark handed to a patron at the time a book check out occurs. And, never forget the power of "buzz" in building demand for a particular library service. Promotion is the final step in matching up the library product with the library customer who wants or needs it.

GOAL SETTING

Library marketing usually begins with questions that match up potential or current resources and those who might benefit from them. What can we do to encourage children to have fun reading? Which of our staff researchers would find this new electronic database of critical help in their offices and labs? What families will benefit from access to a new afterschool homework-help program? How can we best let seniors know about the services we have for them? Such questions show our awareness that libraries aren't the only information source in town anymore. These questions focus on who will benefit, what library service or program will provide this benefit, and how the library can best get its message out to users and potential users. Goal statements also should include how success will be measured or how the library will know that the marketing effort has succeeded.

> Effective marketing begins with creating the right product or service relative to customer needs and wants.

Partnerships

Several of the case studies in this chapter illustrate how libraries make good use of partnerships to promote the library. Library users are members, attendees, and supporters of museums, performing arts, educational and literary organizations. Sharing mailing lists can be an effective method for audience development for cooperating institutions. So, too, can venue sharing, as when library staff read stories at the region's science center or zoo staffers bring small animals to display at a library's family reading festival. The reason for such partnerships is to capture the attention of library non-users to make them aware of library services, and to inform users that their library is trying hard to do its job in imaginative and effective ways. A printed message and logo on a grocery bag or a utility bill carrying the library message is a great way for librarians to get their service and product story before the public at low or no cost. Just as powerful is collaboration with electronic media, restaurants and entertainment venues.

Marketing and Fundraising

A library marketing program is also important because it forms the foundation for the institution as it builds a fundraising culture. Library fundraising begins with institutional development. The base of such development is for a library to market its programs, services and products effectively, thereby creating a vital image in the community. Building friendships, the essence of library development, always finds its beginnings in a successful marketing program.

Marketing Evaluation

The simplest way to evaluate library marketing is to look at its results. Did the marketing program increase registration, circulation, and real or virtual visitation? Did marketing win an increase in funding or attract new donors? Did marketing promote good community feeling toward the library? Marketing assessment criteria should be established before launching a marketing effort. Most libraries will want to project specific changes as part of the goals of the marketing effort. These changes can be quantitative (the library wants to gain 50 new card holders during the outreach program to GED classes). Or the library may want to change attitudes (new academic staff regard the library as helpful because of a library brochure).

In addition to deciding how marketing will be judged, it is important to determine how the evaluation data will be gathered. Should new user records be coded to identify which users obtained new cards as a result of the library's marketing effort? Should users be interviewed or asked to complete a survey? Keep measurement as simple and as accurate as possible. Even if there is no formal evaluation, take time as a staff to gather anecdotal information and consider what produced good results and what did not.

Librarians will also want to analyze the costs in terms of money and staff of marketing efforts to find ways to reduce costs and increase benefits of their marketing efforts.

Many Marketing Options

In the end, remember that the best marketing tool is a satisfied customer. Howard McGinn, head of libraries at Seton Hall University, recognizes that the entire staff is involved in marketing a successful library. He writes:

> New buildings, of course, bring in new customers. The challenge for a library staff is to keep these customers coming back once the novelty of a new facility has worn off. Our marketing effort had to be constructed in a manner that brought faculty and students into the building while creating a foundation that would make them want to return. I use the term "effort" and not "plan" deliberately. It has been my experience that formal marketing plans are most useful when the products or services are established and significant sums of money are involved or when new products are being introduced at a significant expense. Marketing plans for libraries often introduce a needless layer of bureaucracy that most often gives administrators reasons NOT to do something. Management and staff must have flexibility in forming marketing efforts in order to respond quickly to opportunities and/or problems that require a marketing solution.[3]

The most effective libraries draw from the full range of promotional and advertising tools available. They publicize their offerings with programs, exhibitions, product displays, counter cards, bookmarks, posters, service lists, path finders, bibliographies and virtual and physical catalogs. They advertise on- and off-site; in yellow-page listings, newspapers and magazines; radio and television, on billboards, on public buses and on their own library work vehicles. They look for public service announcements in every medium. They use electronic postings, e-mail, blogs and RSS feeds.

A library marketing program is also important because it forms the foundation for the institution as it builds a fundraising culture.

Within this context, the case studies in this section are examples of different types of libraries organizing imaginative and effective marketing and communication campaigns to connect their institutions' resources with constituencies they wanted to reach.

These case studies show that effective library marketing is innovative, persistent and cost conscious. It should be innovative, because libraries serve so many markets. It should be persistent, because the library market is always reorganizing itself into different configurations. And, it must be cost conscious. The case studies also show how adaptive library marketing can be. Libraries that operate in very different settings, varied financial conditions and with very diverse constituencies can all develop successful marketing and outreach programs.

The Wilton (CT) Library Association quickly created a unique program to deal with a disturbing community incident. Wilton's public library reacted to homophobic and racist slurs on high school lockers, leading community groups, faith organizations and media representatives in organizing community discussion groups built around six films about prejudice and tolerance. The programs affirmed the public library's core role in furthering democracy, won an unanticipated award from the Connecticut Library Association, increased donations to the library's capital fund and helped keep the library "on the town's radar screen."

First Regional Library Cooperative in Hernando, MS appealed to its youth market by creating "Info Family" to promote its "Plug into the Power of Your Public Library" campaign. The library's four-member, super-hero family – Captain Info, Storyteller, Page and Dewey – drawn in graphic-novel style and used on everything from the website to T-shirts and bookmarks, gained a huge following among the young – and help publicize the library's services.

Houston Public Library also appealed to youth with its "Power Card Challenge." This marketing and branding initiative reached out to Houston's diverse population groups, increasing juvenile library registrations to hundreds of area children. The campaign strengthened the library's relationships with community groups and schools as well.

INFOhio (The Information Network for Ohio Schools) produced a professional four-minute video and added content to the organization's website to alert parents to the enormous resources the network hosted on its website. The video has enjoyed wide viewing, increasing awareness of the resources for teachers and students as well.

We hope that these illustrations of marketing and outreach success will help you consider and carry out your own successful efforts.

ENDNOTES

[1] Christine M. Koontz. "Customer-Based Marketing. Stores and Libraries: Both Serve Customers!" MLS. *Marketing Library Services*. Volume 16, No. 1. Jan/Feb 2002. Downloaded on April 29, 2006 from http://www.infotoday.com/mls/jan02/koontz.htm.

[2] Christine M. Koontz. "Section on Management and Marketing. Glossary of Marketing Definitions" IFLANET 1998. Downloaded on April 29, 2006 from http://www.ifla.org/VII/s34/pubs/glossary.htm#M.

[3] Howard F. McGinn. "Getting Started: Case Histories. Carlson Library, Clarion University." *ALA (American Library Association) Public Information Office, Campaign for American Libraries. Academic and Research Libraries Campaign*. Downloaded on April 28, 2006 from http://www.ala.org/ala/pio/campaign/academicresearch/successfulacademic.htm.

BIBLIOGRAPHY

Kotler, Philip. *Marketing Management: Analysis, Planning, Implementation and Control*. (8th Edition, Englewood Cliffs, NJ; Prentice-Hall, 1997).

Rao, V.O. & Steckel, J.H. "Segmenting Markets: Who Are the Potential Buyers." *Analysis for Strategic Marketing*. (Reading, MA: Addison-Wesley, 1998).

CASE STUDY: GEORGIA INSTITUTE OF TECHNOLOGY, ATLANTA, GA

"We're viewing the library as not merely a place to check out books, but a place to support all student study and student activities."

Lori Critz
Reference and Subject Librarian
Georgia Institute of Technology
Library and Information Center

Challenges

- Show incoming students the importance and scope of the library, and make the library a "crossroad" for students on campus

Solutions

- Host gaming night the first weekend in the fall to introduce freshmen to library facilities and resources

- Become part of Recently Acquired Tech Students (RATS) Week orientation and invite campus groups to participate

Benefits

- Students recognize library as a valuable resource and a friendly place as proven through survey and focus group responses, as well as strong, active participation in library events

OVERVIEW

In 2004, the Library staff at the Georgia Institute of Technology (Georgia Tech) wanted to strengthen its relationship with students on campus, especially the student organizations. They also wanted to make a stronger impression on incoming students, and make them aware of what the Library offers, hoping to present the Library and Information Center as a destination for both academic support and campus activities.

The Library joined a long standing campus program called "RATS Week" (Recently Acquired Tech Students) by hosting its own event, "RATS in the Library." The event welcomed first-years for a night of games, music, live performances, and prizes, helping them become familiar with the Library surroundings and staff. The Library created strong ties with many student clubs on campus and demonstrated that in Georgia Tech's academically competitive environment, the library encouraged a balance between academic and social pursuits. As a result of Library staff efforts, many more Tech students see the Library as both a prominent and convenient academic resource, and a campus gathering place.

CHALLENGE

Georgia Tech has a combined population of 16,500 undergraduate and graduate students, with approximately 2,800 incoming freshmen each year. In recent years, Library administrators recognized that the Library needed to gain more visibility for its academic services and status as a gathering place for students to meet, study and socialize. "Our main objective," says librarian Lori Critz, "was to put the Library in the forefront of students' minds. We wanted to heighten the Library's profile as a place to gather, work together, and socialize."

SOLUTION

In 2004, the Library chose a long-standing university orientation as its higher profile coming out party. Each August, at the start of the academic year, Georgia Tech hosts "RATS Week." RATS, or Recently Acquired Tech Students, spend the first week attending information sessions, and activities where they meet other students and learn about campus organizations. The week is organized by FASET (Familiarization and Adaptation to the Surroundings and Environs of Tech), a student group responsible for helping RATS learn about campus life and organizations of interest.

Beginning in May, three months prior to RATS Week, the Library began planning "RATS in the Library." Reference and Subject Librarian Lori Critz, joined Crit Stuart, associate director for public services, Richard Meyer, the dean of libraries, and campus groups to craft "a night of gaming, library information, films, music, and theater."

Participating organizations, including the Office of Information and Technology (OIT), were eager to work with the Library. Each contributed from its bank of staff skills. OIT, for example, contributed an estimated 200 hours mainly in programming and computer server preparation. The Library contributed about 100 hours. "Our preparation focused on event organization and marketing," Critz explains. FASET and the library promoted the night on the university's website, in flyers, and also in freshman orientation packets.

The inaugural "RATS in the Library" event took place on Saturday, August 21, 2004. The main attraction that evening was the Unreal Tournament LAN Party, a videogame competition held in the library media center. Ninety-three freshmen competed, and the tournament winner received a 20GB iPod. Semifinalists won 256MB SanDisk Flash Drives and T-shirts. Other library events that night included performances by Georgia Tech's Improvisation Troupe, Let's Try This!, songs by three on-campus a capella groups, movies sponsored by the Anime Club and GT Campus MovieFest. The campus radio station rounded out the entertainment.

While the students enjoyed the festivities, they learned about the Library and its role as a campus destination. The entire night, students were able to see and use all the Library has to offer. Students playing video games could see that the new technology lab, Library West Commons, enabled students to create web pages, edit videos, and work on class presentations. All around the Library, posters advertised resources, including information classes taught by librarians, and information librarian expertise.

All told, 40 to 50 Library staff members volunteered at the RATS event, and total costs of approximately $3 thousand paid for event food, advertising, and prizes.

Benefits

At the conclusion of the orientation week, first years completed surveys and gave "RATS in the Library" high marks. Critz, Stuart, and the rest of the library staff used this feedback to develop subsequent orientations and conduct several student focus groups. Consistently, requests came in for more library information/social evenings. "Students want more," Critz explains, "not just more gaming, but anything that would let them come in on a Friday or Saturday night and use the Library as a campus crossroad."

The program also proved to be a great library networking tool, giving staff an opportunity to collaborate with other organizations on campus, and strengthen ties with student groups. "I do a lot of the instructional sessions," Critz points out, "and students come in and say, 'I know you!' They remember me as a friendly face."

This year's plan for "RATS in the Library" builds on past success, with the promise of new attractions and participation opportunities.

CASE STUDY: INFORMATION NETWORK FOR OHIO SCHOOLS, (INFOhio), COLUMBUS, OH

"Our greatest challenge is to increase awareness of what INFOhio has to offer, especially among our parents, but also for teachers and students."

Ann E. Tepe
Special Projects Consultant
INFOhio

Challenges

• Create ways to increase awareness of INFOhio's resources specifically for parents of preK-12 students

• Create professional tools and enhanced website content for parents, school librarians and teachers, while remaining within grant funding constraints

Solutions

• Created a project team from the school library and educational communities

• Surveyed parent focus groups about their understanding of INFOhio and how to increase use

• Created a video on what INFOhio has to offer the community. Posted the video on the website for easy parent/teacher access

Benefits

• Positive feedback to the video has increased interest in and awareness of INFOhio's resources

• Exposure to INFOhio's resources has increased via delivery of their new, 37-page booklet to school librarians: Toolkit for Promoting INFOhio Resources to Parents

OVERVIEW

According to their website, INFOhio, the Information Network For Ohio (K-12) Schools "...is a statewide cooperative project to create an electronic network linking Ohio students, teachers, library/media specialists and others via computer to:

• School libraries in the same district and across the state.
• College and University libraries through cooperative efforts with OhioLINK (the academic library network).
• Public and special libraries through cooperative efforts with OPLIN (the public library network)."

Ann Tepe, special projects consultant for INFOhio (a former educator and school librarian) says, "INFOhio provides all Ohio public and nonpublic schools with a core collection of online resources, which is age-appropriate, curriculum-related, and designed to complement Ohio's Academic Content Standards."

CHALLENGE

"One of our biggest challenges at INFOhio has been to widen the scope of student, teacher and parent awareness of INFOhio's core of free resources," according to Ann. The INFOhio Governing Advisory Board also wanted to add content for the parent audience to INFOhio's website (http://www.infohio.org). A grant was needed in order to accomplish this two-fold goal, which came from The Reinberger Foundation in Cleveland, Ohio. Once the grant was awarded to INFOhio, the clock began ticking. They had one year to analyze parent needs and determine how best to utilize the grant money.

SOLUTION

The primary task involved surveying over 50 parents among ten focus groups, representing over 100 students from rural, urban and suburban areas. Home-schooled, private and public school students from all districts were represented. Each parent completed a two-page form which included questions about home computers, whether they helped their children with their homework, and if not, who did. Ann Tepe conducted all of the focus group interviews and from them she learned that many parents had Internet access and knew of INFOhio but had never used it. Many had seen mention of a single INFOhio resource cited by teachers in their childrens' homework assignments, but had not delved further into the fourteen other resources available from INFOhio.

A project team was created, drawing on strong relationships with the Ohio Educational Library Media Association and other school library organizations. Based on overwhelming feedback from parents citing the need to promote the electronic resources available from INFOhio, it was decided that the grant money would go toward three important tools: first, a video to be posted on the website to explain what INFOhio is, touching on the many resources and services available, second, an initiative to "beef up" the parent web page content, and third, a toolkit to help school librarians promote INFOhio, especially to parents.

A four minute video was created by a professional video company, Glazen Studios of Cleveland, which had experience working with libraries. Glazen and INFOhio collaborated on the collection of interviews with parents, administrators, school librarians and students who described, on camera, the benefits of using INFOhio's resources, such as its high quality, educator-selected resources, alignment with national and Ohio educational standards, and reading level designations for teachers to use in determining its relevancy to individual student's needs.

BENEFITS

"Feedback on the video has been overwhelmingly positive," said Ann. "We had requests even before the video was released." Use of the video has become popular for parent teacher conference nights, at school board meetings, and as a start to school presentations. Here is a link to the "What is INFOhio?" video, which is now also available in DVD and VHS formats:

http://www.infohio.org/Parent/OutreachKit/Video2005.html

The successful video project gave way to another initiative, leveraging INFOhio's collaborative relationship with vendors to create downloadable INFOhio screen savers for school computers. Enlisting the help of marketing specialists from EBSCO Publishing and other vendors, INFOhio brainstormed communication and distribution solutions that would promote INFOhio's website resources, in a manner both appealing and cost effective. The animated screensavers developed as a direct result of those sessions.

Downloadable from the INFOhio website, they feature a "Think INFOhio" tag line that appeals to students, teachers, and parents.

"INFOhio has an abundance of excellent resources on its website," explains Scott Bernier, the director of communications at EBSCO Publishing. "The goal is to guide users to the site, where they can take advantage of those resources," he continues. "Ann Tepe and her colleagues take a forward-thinking, collaborative approach to communication. They enlist feedback from users, as well as new perspectives and expertise from vendor partners, to better promote INFOhio's resources, and to better serve Ohio's school community," he explains.

INFOhio also created a 37-page booklet for school librarians, which included bookmarks, posters, playing cards and sample newsletter articles about INFOhio's resources. Funding needed to print and distribute (via mail and delivery by state Information Technology Centers) this booklet was provided with the help of the Institute for Library and Information Literacy Education, ILILE, at Kent State University. Every public and nonpublic school in Ohio has received a copy of the booklet and, according to Ann, "our focus group parents volunteered to hand deliver copies to their school superintendents. They wanted to be sure their school districts were using INFOhio." In the short time since the books were distributed (February 2006), feedback has been very positive, measured by increased website counts and positive feedback from parents and school librarians, as well as increased teacher awareness and resource utilization in homework assignments. INFOhio is transforming teaching and learning in Ohio by helping school libraries and librarians do their job. INFOhio exists as a tool for librarians to help students learn and teachers teach. And, it is a critical resource for parents, according to Ann. "Common sense tells us and research shows that when parents are involved in a child's education, the student generally has higher grades, higher test scores, better attendance, and more consistent and completed homework. That's why going forward, INFOhio will continue to promote the use of their rich electronic resources to parents by working directly with school librarians, their vital link to teaching in Ohio."

Figure 1.
Opening page of the "Think INFOhio" promotional screen saver

CASE STUDY: HOUSTON PUBLIC LIBRARY, HOUSTON, TX

"We knew it was a matter of paying close attention
to demographics and making a connection."

Andrea Lapsley
Assistant Director
Marketing & Development
Houston Public Library

Challenges

• Reach all local demographics to increase juvenile library registrations by 30 percent

• Market the initiative to appeal to kids as well as other members in the community

• Increase the Library's identity within the community

Solutions

• Take proactive measures to extend the Library into the community and the school district

• Create and implement successful branding and marketing techniques

• Develop and foster partnerships with other organizations and institutions within the community

Benefits

• Over 300,000 Houston area children are proud to own and use a library card

• Library serves as a model for others to follow

• Library has a renewed identity and increased visibility within the community

OVERVIEW

The Houston Public Library was not expecting Mayor Lee P. Brown to publicly dedicate his administration to the children of Houston and the importance of reading and libraries, during his inauguration. Brown's message was simple: to encourage children to read, it is imperative that every child in Houston own a library card. However, the mayor's comments were only the beginning of the Library staff's major three-year marketing and public relations campaign ahead.

Known as the "Power Card Challenge," the campaign pledged to increase juvenile registration from all local demographics, using proactive marketing and community outreach techniques. The initiative aimed to involve everyone in the public including adults and staff who were excited to follow the Library's slogan, "Pack the Power." The Library established strong local partnerships and increased its identity as an essential and accessible institution within the Houston community. Over the life of this three-year project, from June, 1998 to June, 2001, the Library gradually achieved the cardholder and circulation goals they had set at each branch, ultimately tripling the number of juvenile cardholders in the Houston area, from 100,000 to over 300,000, and increasing juvenile circulation more than 30 percent.

Challenge

As the Houston Public Library began planning for the Power Card Challenge in 1998, research showed that of the 512,717 children living in the library-serving area, fewer then 25 percent held library cards. Further complicating matters was the reality that Houston's Hispanic population was the most under-served by the library in relation to those numbers. "We couldn't just expect that kids were going to come walking through our doors," says Andrea Lapsley, Assistant Director of Marketing for the Houston Public Library. "We knew it was a matter of paying close attention to demographics and making a connection." To effectively address those two issues, the Library needed to fashion a card registration promotion that would appeal to children, and keep them coming to the Library.

Solutions

First, the Library arranged with the school district to include a public library card application in the packet each child received on the first day of school. This not only emphasized to children that the card is an academic necessity, but also showed it is easy to obtain. Lapsley reveals, "We realized that we had to take the Library into the community. We worked very closely with the school district, but we also manned sign-up booths at other off-site locations such as the rodeo, the petting zoo, grocery stores, malls, museums and cultural institutions." She stresses that the heart of the campaign was establishing fruitful partnerships and finding new ways of communicating the Library's message.

The lead sponsor for the campaign became the local power company, Reliant Energy, Inc™, which generously funded design of the energetic, eye-catching, Power Card Challenge logo, and included Power Card information in their bill inserts. "We literally called the power company and said, 'We have a unique and special opportunity for you,'" says Lapsley. But the library reached out to numerous other corporations for their support, and eventually partnered with over 300 organizations that were able to lend their support and help raise money. Hispanic media outlets were also eager to show their support and contributed to 33 percent of the campaign's media coverage.

While children were the initial focus of the Power Card Challenge, it became increasingly clear that all members of the library staff and the community, young and old, could get involved. Lapsley reflects, "The staff was so energized by this activity. It was a lot of fun, and it gave them something creative to focus on." By openly welcoming many active participants, the Library now had a major force within the community with their hearts set on success.

Benefits

Despite the struggles inherent in any three-year campaign, the Houston Public Library experienced numerous successes. Children felt invited and more comfortable using the library resources. The "Tower of Power," a ten foot stack of faux books in the Library's lobby with a measuring eye known as the "critter" made its way quickly up the stack to show the climb in number of cardholders. Monthly reports tracked registration increases, and numeric and demographic registration goals were met. "We really just saw everything go up across the board," says Lapsley.

With a renewed and powerful identity in the community, the Houston Public Library is proud to serve as a model for other libraries. It continues to field inquiries about resources needed to replicate the campaign, and Lapsley stresses that a community short on funding should not be discouraged. Even following only some aspects of the program will yield success. "The basic premise was: The Library is there to serve the community. From there we partnered with the schools, corporations, and cultural organizations to help get our message out." She adds that establishing these partnerships with dedicated and enthusiastic members of the community helps to propagate money, media coverage, free printing, and donated time. "Supporting the Library will touch everyone in the community," Lapsley reflects, "but it is the library's responsibility to make a personal connection when patrons come in."

CASE STUDY: FIRST REGIONAL LIBRARY, HERNANDO, MS

"We believe in marketing and we've seen it pay off. We've created a fun, good vibe with the local kids. They're talking about it, they're coming in, and they're logging on to our website."

Victoria Penny
Early Childhood Coordinator
First Regional Library

Challenges

• Generate interest in reading and the library among teenagers

• Increase cardholding among pre-teens, especially boys

• Promote library services, technologies and electronic resources to local and rural areas via library website and branches

Solutions

• Rolled out "Info Family" library campaign with superhero theme

• Launched extensive marketing program in conjunction with National Library Week

• Promoted federated searching through character tales

Benefits

• Increased library traffic & positioned website as the "14th branch"

• Attracted target audience to reading

• Built teamwork and enthusiasm among library staff and strong relationships with the community

OVERVIEW

In April 2005, the First Regional Library Cooperative launched Info Family, an original marketing initiative inspired by superhero characters from the graphic novel and comic book genres. Developed to promote the library's "Plug into the Power of Your Public Library" campaign, First Regional Library's Info Family features prominently on the library website, and on-site at the cooperative's 13 branches. The campaign successfully met three library goals: promote library resources and services in the community, expand usage among teens and young boys, and boost the use of electronic resources, especially among rural library patrons.

Says Early Childhood Coordinator Victoria Penny, "We believe in marketing and we've seen it pay off. We've created a fun, good vibe with the local kids. They're talking about it, they're coming in, and they're logging on to our website." To visit the First Regional Library website, go to http://www.first.lib.ms.us/.

CHALLENGE

The Info Family initiative took shape when two interests found a common cause. First Regional Library Public Relations Specialist David Brown valued the appeal of graphic novels with teens and children, and hoped to apply the theme for library promotion. Catherine Nathan, the Library's new director, was looking for a vehicle to launch the Library's "Plug into the Power of the Public Library" campaign for National Library Week. First Lady Laura Bush's public comments[1] about the need for effective library programs to interest boys in reading[2] further fueled Nathan's idea to promote the Library in the community. Together, Nathan and Brown settled on a promotion featuring original graphic novel superheroes to market the effort.

SOLUTION – A TIMELINE

With $15,000 in grant monies from LSTA, $3,750 in local matching funds, and revenue from the Library's own publicity budget, Brown created an original design of Captain Info, Storyteller, Page, and Dewey – Info Family – a family of four superheroes, plus a library website to host the initiative. Each Info Family member's superpower highlights a library resource skill, from database searching to finding favorite stories or book research. Captain Info anchors catalog and article database searching. Page promotes teen patron offerings. Dewey guides patrons to resources for children. Storyteller offers access to the library newsletter, and highlights information about library events, branch locations, and general library information. Brown, Nathan, and Youth Services Coordinator Victoria Penny, developed a business plan and promotion schedule for rollout to the public during National Library Week in April 2005. Info Family Rollout Promotional Materials included:

- T-shirts for library staff

- A full color, cinema-style standing cutout of Info Family for each branch

- Stickers featuring the four different Info Family heroes, for schools and public library branches

- Spring 2005 issue of "What's Happening" library newsletter dedicated to the campaign

- February 2005 – Brown presented a promotional poster to the 13 regional branch librarians. The poster featured the Info Family in silhouette only, with the tease tag line "Coming Soon to a Library Near You" to build interest in the event.

- March 2005 – The Info Family Librarian Launch. Brown, Nathan and Penny outlined and discussed all elements of the program and promotion in a launch meeting with branch librarians. Brown unveiled the Library's Info Family website and a standing marquee cutout. Local newspapers interviewed Catherine Nathan, and jumped on the Info Family story. They dedicated front page coverage to the initiative in a story published prior to National Library Week.

- April 2005 – Info Family Public Launch. Branch librarians began the public education program, promoted the website, and distributed stickers and bookmarks. Responding to the publicity, families flooded in. Children requested photos standing next to the Info Family illustration, which was published in the local paper. Brown taught "Superhero" drawing classes that introduced children to the basics of drawing with a superhero theme, encouraging individual creativity and artistic expression.

BENEFITS

According to Nathan, a coordinated effort between First Regional as the public library and the school libraries in various counties amplified the initiative's message to the students and their parents. "Our collaboration with school libraries helped create a buzz among children." The school libraries received pre-launch information along with the branch libraries, and they conveyed it to students during library time. "Students were talking about it on the playground at recess," Nathan continues. "Then it took off. What began as an appeal to the 'Gamer' or 'millennial' generation of elementary school-age children, is now a 21st century hit across all age groups in the community."

As evidence of their popularity, Penny reports that new library cards featuring Info Family are in demand, and adults are already asking to exchange their old cards for the fun and colorful Info Family cards. Moreover, with Info Family, the First Regional Library has used its own intellectual property and become an active player in the life of the community it serves. More boys, girls and adults are coming to the library in person or in cyberspace, asking about its programs and website.

"The enthusiasm shown in just the first two months since launch has given us the green light to pursue our goals," says Nathan. "We want our website to be our 14th bona fide branch. Our electronic resources and federated searching tools are fantastic." In April 2006 the Library unveiled a redesigned website promoting those resources, organizing them by Info Family skill. For example, by clicking Captain Info, the library's online patrons can peruse the iBistro, a suite of tools that includes catalog searching, and Find it Fast topic searching for 28 subjects in the adult section of the Library, each set off by a colorful icon heading. The Children's Library iBistro features 15 searchable subject headings. The suite also displays links from the main catalog to the Library's Recommended Reading and Best Seller lists from the *New York Times* and *Publishers Weekly*. http://frlsirsi.first.lib.ms.us/uhtbin/cgisirsi/x/0/0/49/.

Nathan continues, "Using monics now available to us, we'll organize Info Family youth focus groups to develop themed coloring and activity books." She will also use Info Family to promote the library's summer reading programs.

According to David Brown, there have been some unexpected rewards as well – celebrity. "Two young kids came up, and one pointed at me and said to the other, 'He's the one who made Info Family.' They wanted to have their picture taken with me. It was priceless!"

ENDNOTES

[1] Lyric Wallwork Winik. "We Need To Pay More Attention To Boys."
    PARADE Magazine, January 16, 2005.

[2] "The statistics are consistent: Young male readers lag behind their female counterparts.
    According to the Progress in International Reading Literacy Study (PIRLS) in 2001, fourth-grade girls in all of the 30 plus participating countries scored higher in reading literacy than fourth-grade boys by a statistically significant amount. Similar findings show up in the U.S. National Assessment of Educational Progress (NAEP) scores, as well as in studies in New Zealand, England, Wales, Scotland, and Northern Ireland." from "Boys and Books," by Jane McFann, Reading Today, August/September 2004 International Reading Association website http://www.reading.org/.

CAPTAIN INFO

At last!!!

A hero who fights to make information available to all...

CAPTAIN INFO!

Captain Info's "super brain" can filter through millions of books, bibliographies, reference sites, and informational databases to obtain the answers to ANY question at lightning speed!

Captain Info and his wife, Storyteller, along with their children Page and Dewey, are...**The INFO FAMILY!**

STORYTELLER

STORYTELLER

The beautiful wife, mother, and superhero STORYTELLER is a living, breathing, storybook! All the world's stories, legends and tales are at her command! Storyteller's powers go beyond being able to tell any story, however...

With a wave of her hand, Storyteller can create lifelike images in the air which fully illustrate her spellbinding tales!

PAGE

PAGE

At first glance, PAGE seems like a "typical teenager," but she is so much more! Page inherited her father's "encyclopedic knowledge" and can also find the answer to ANY question! This young lady has her own gifts as well! If you're looking for info on movies, music, trends, or any other "Pop Culture" topic, Page is the go-to-girl! Page is also a "super reader," devouring dozens of books a day-- and she's always ready to recommend books to fellow teens!

DEWEY

DEWEY

This rambunctious 10 year old is full of energy...and just a little bit of mischief! His dad, Captain Info, created a special helmet for Dewey which harnesses all that energy and helps him locate ANY book, anywhere, anytime, anyplace! Dewey is learning more and more everyday about what it means to be an INFORMATION SUPERHERO, and how important it is to make sure information is available to everyone!

"Operation Respect fashioned a silver lining from the cloud of a shocking incident. Through it, we affirmed the public library's responsibility to provide a venue for civil discourse, and seized an incredible opportunity to gather and to learn from others in a very personal way. People now truly think of Wilton Library as their library. They view it as an institution integrally involved and responsive to the needs of our community."

Kathy Leeds
Director
Wilton Library

Challenges

- Incident of homophobic and racist slurs defacing lockers at the high school

- Generate funds for major library expansion and renovation

Solutions

- 'Operation Respect' community-wide film discussion series coordinated by the Library

- Total cost $800, excluding new projector

- Operation Respect unexpectedly opened up new funding sources and grant monies

Benefits

- 'Operation Respect' has made Wilton Library a focal point for community pride and an example to other public libraries and community organizations across the country

- Private donations and grants exceeded original capital funding targets by $2 million

- Community efforts recognized by Connecticut Library Association

Overview

Wilton Library in Wilton, Connecticut, is a public library serving a community of 18,000 residents, and is run by a private library association. Its annual operating budget is $2.3 million. The town provides $1.8 million, and the association must raise the remaining $500,000. Additionally, in 2002, it embarked on a capital campaign to fund a library building expansion project, with an estimated $3.2 million in private funding required.

In 2004, the Library served as a catalyst for community action in response to a racial incident at the local high school. The Library proposed 'Operation Respect', a six-week film discussion series with facilitators as the perfect vehicle to bring people together," says Kathy Leeds, director of Wilton Library. The program was open to all ages, free of charge, and met with universal support and enthusiasm.

Operation Respect brought Wilton Library to "the top of the heap" of public pride and awareness, and garnered an award from the Connecticut Library Association. In addition to boosting regular annual fundraising, the effort generated unexpected funds for a library building campaign. In 2004-2005 private donations and previously untapped grant sources supplied funds that surpassed initial goals by more than $2 million. According to Leeds, "There is no doubt that the figure reflects awareness of Operation Respect at the Wilton Library, and its role as a gathering place for diverse exchange and respectful dialogue."

Challenge

Wilton was stunned when authorities discovered racist and homophobic slurs defacing lockers at the high school. Within days, representatives from the public library, the high school, religious congregations, municipal government, and youth organizations gathered at a roundtable meeting to fashion a proactive response.

During the response meeting, the superintendent of schools offered the name Operation Respect. "Everyone loved it," says Leeds. "It was so fitting. It focused on affirming a core value, and more appropriately than the word 'tolerance'."

Solution/Response

Energized, Leeds tapped the strong network of community contacts she has nurtured over the years, seeking perspectives on different types of discrimination. The response was immediate. "We knew we needed to move quickly. I called six people, and all six said, 'we'll be there.' They'd all had some experience of discrimination's injury, and were helpful in selecting films to show," she adds.

In just a few weeks, the program was in place. The facilitators came from the Wilton community: a member of the Board of Education committed to multicultural education discussed hate crimes and discrimination. A member of the Board of Finance and president of a nonprofit agency discussed social class and prejudice. The fire commissioner discussed the impact of September 11th and the Patriot Act on Arabs, Muslims, and Southeast Asians. A rabbi discussed anti-Semitism. An Episcopal priest facilitated dialogue about homophobia. The dean of Middlebrook School, Wilton's middle school, and a supporter of the A Better Chance (ABC) program, led a discussion of racism and sexism. Open to all ages, free of charge: six leaders, six films, six weeks. It was Wilton's lucky number.

The program was simple: come to the Library, watch a film, then discuss it and listen with your heart. "Community organizations helped defray expenses, including the purchase of films," continues Leeds.

"Local press and media organizations publicized the initiative. We sent out postcards to all residents. Hundreds attended, students, teachers and adults alike, and the discussions were sincere and soul searching."

BENEFITS

In February 2005, the Connecticut State Library Association bestowed "The Connecticut Award for Excellence in Public Library Service" on Wilton's Library Association. In its notification letter, the awards committee commented that one judge considered Operation Respect an emblem of the best of what a public library can do and stands for.

There were unexpected windfalls too, namely a marked increase in private contributions to the Library's building fund. Leeds' philosophy and approach are the same for both library fundraising and community advocacy. "Our goal as a library institution is to stay on the town's radar screen. We've taken the time to develop community relationships, with the municipal government, schools, and the business community. We take nothing for granted."

In the fall and winter of 2004/2005, other programs developed in the spirit of Operation Respect:

- A program on homophobia
- An international book discussion group
- A community-wide read of "To Kill a Mockingbird"
- A collaboration with Norwalk Community College to present a program on the Holocaust and the American Civil Rights Movement

Reflecting on Wilton Library's award-winning program, Kathy Leeds offers some final words. "In presenting our story, I want to emphasize that ours is not a solution, because prejudice is not an isolated incident. It's widespread. Ours is an ongoing, proactive and dedicated response, an effort to raise awareness, to encourage further programming and inspire other libraries to follow our lead."

[1] ALA has many marketing initiatives that can be accessed by visiting the ALA website (www.ala.org). Most divisions have marketing campaigns, sections or committees and marketing publications. ALA also has supporting information for its "@your library" marketing initiative.

[2] *Library Marketing—Thinking Outside the Book (Blog)*. (http://librarymarketing.blogspot.com/) Ohio Library Council.

This is an excellent source of ideas and discussion of library marketing techniques and issues.

[3] Fisher, Patricia and Marseilla Pride. *Blueprint for Your Library Marketing Plan: A Guide to Help You Survive and Thrive*. (Chicago: ALA, 2005).

Walters, Suzanne. Library Marketing That Works! (New York: Neal-Schuman, April 2004).

Both Fisher and Pride and Walters provide practical advice for librarians with library specific information.

[4] Kotler, Philip. *Principles of Marketing (11th Edition)*. (Englewood Cliffs, NJ: Prentice-Hall, 2005).

This provides theories and basic information from the marketing profession.

WORSHEET

GETTING STARTED

If you want to start a marketing program at your library, redirect the program you have, or add a little more life to your existing marketing program, here are some steps to take to get started:

1. Review recent marketing efforts at your library. Identify what is being done, what works and what doesn't work.

_____

_____

_____

_____

_____

_____

2. Conduct research. Check with similar libraries. Read, and talk to other local nonprofits to see what marketing techniques have worked. Talk to your staff to come up with new ideas. Identify five or six new marketing activities you'd like to try.

_____

_____

_____

_____

_____

_____

3. Describe your new marketing program, list possible activities and set goals. Identify target audience (s).

_____

_____

_____

_____

_____

_____

4. How will you know your marketing effort has been successful? How will you evaluate your marketing project?

_____

_____

_____

_____

_____

_____

5. Identify what expertise you will need to carry out your marketing plan. Where will you obtain these skills? (Library staff, paid consultants, pro bono help from advertising agencies or media outlets, etc.)

_____

_____

_____

_____

_____

_____

6. What is the budget for your marketing program? How will you get the money you need to support the program?

_____

_____

_____

_____

_____

_____

PARTNERSHIP
AND COLLABORATION

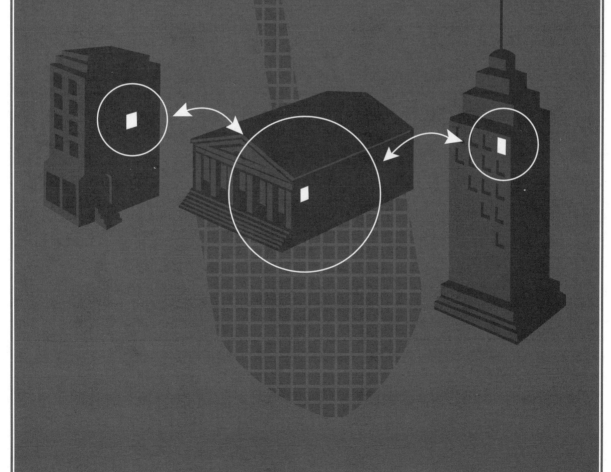

Prospecting for Partnerships

Partnerships begin for libraries the same way that gold seekers search for wealth: they start with prospecting. Management sets the prospecting tone by defining how widely the library will spread the partnership prospecting net and how tightly partnership conditions have to be met before allocating resources. Savvy and knowledgeable library staff are great prospectors. Every staff member belongs to a network that extends beyond the library. Openness to partnership ideas from unexpected sources is a hallmark of an opportunistic manager.

> Savvy and knowledgeable library staff are great prospectors. Every staff member is part of networks other than those in the library.

Strong libraries have this component, and tend to have more collaborative opportunities than they can develop; other libraries may have to work hard to obtain their initial partnerships. Libraries with a weak resource base should be mindful that a successful collaboration may absorb resources that are needed to support basic services required to carry out the institutional mission.

Libraries find opportunities for partnerships all around them. Strong organizations want to collaborate with strong libraries because they recognize the myriad resources that libraries can bring to the table. Examples include expert children's storytelling in a zoo children's festival and the library's local history specialists to partner with an art museum to organize a database on regional art and artists. Weak organizations want partnerships with strong libraries in order to access to their resources to help them do their jobs. Examples include a campus organization asking its institutional library to prepare a program at a monthly meeting in order to meet a student union funding requirement, or a school system asking the public library to assume school library responsibilities.

Types of library partnerships

Library partnerships usually fall into one of the following types:

Training. As libraries adapt, they need training not available on staff. For example, when libraries adopt new computer software or hardware, they seek relevant instruction from nearby colleges, other campus departments and communication companies in return for offering free library cards, expanded services or delivery to a partner's principal facility.

Funding. Partners fund innovative library programs, provide publicity through print and electronic advertisements, money to support campaigns in lieu of public funding and pro bono skills. In return, they receive recognition of association with an effective, high visibility, public-service organization working to improve the quality of community life. Some businesses have goals for donations to community groups and value libraries as partners that give strong outcome returns for the business dollar invested.

> Libraries find opportunities for partnerships all around them. Strong organizations want to collaborate with libraries because they recognize the myriad resources that libraries have to offer.

Research and its dissemination. Partner libraries compile, author, fact-check and field-test information that is published by a print or electronic vendor. The publisher earns the income from the project, and the library receives free copies of the publication, and gains status in the profession for collaborating to improve reference sources. Such research and dissemination partnerships may include libraries and museums, libraries and university departments, or libraries and government agencies. They can involve supporting research from collections, publishing of guides or encyclopedias or operating an electronic website for an entire service district, region or state.

Program development. In this kind of partnership, the partners share expertise, publicity costs and the audiences who come to the programs. For example, a public library and a school system can work together to improve student outcomes such as developing reading skills and improving test results. Other examples include: a library working with a health care agency to organize neighborhood health information programs, a library and a campus YMCA operating a homework help program, or a library and a professional theater, music or art program for young audiences.

Building audiences. A library could partner with a professional sports team to give away game tickets to reading achievers and their parents. Both the library and the sports team gain audiences. A library could collaborate with a television or radio station to organize special theater appreciation discussion programs involving college and high school students who attend special showings of a university repertoire theater. All the lives touched are enriched, and audiences learn about other opportunities to learn and appreciate.

Sharing audiences. Libraries share current audiences with bookstores for jointly sponsored book talks. Libraries share their users with booksellers when they encourage those who want to buy books to use that vendor so that the library will receive some of the revenue from the purchase. Reciprocal lending programs between university campuses in a region or among libraries within a state or metropolitan area are examples of sharing audiences in order to serve all of them better.

Sharing space. Many libraries share spaces with community recreation centers, student unions and theaters. It is not unusual to find a public library operating as part of a school library or vice versa. Libraries today also are found in shopping centers and government centers. Usually such space-sharing arrangements work out, saving money and providing access to greater numbers of patrons. However, disparate schedules, audience settings, and patterns of use can present shared-space problems that should be considered before agreements are signed.

Sharing staff expertise. As libraries learn to take full advantage of electronic resources, staff members will find it easier to communicate and share knowledge. For example, EBSCO's *NoveList* and *NextReads* services both offer accumulated expertise from several libraries, shared among many libraries at the same time. Utilizing these services, local librarians can tailor the product received from the vendor in a unique way to better meet the needs of local customers.

Political alliances. Many libraries are not allowed to lobby in order to pass, fight or retain library legislation or tax initiatives. Partners may be willing to help when such activity is prohibited or highly limited. One example is when a financial firm that organizes bond sales agrees to do the lobbying for a bond issue to assist a particular library. Another example is when many public libraries get together to improve their administrative status by hiring a lobbyist to bring about a change in state law. Finally, school library staff may join teachers organizations in lobbying for improved funding for public schools, including more funding for school libraries.

Plan, organize, resource, and manage partnerships

The most important element in success is for the collaborating institutions to be clear on what they need from each other and in what they have to give in return. Select the organization that is the most likely to share the library's view of the project at hand; one with a staff interested in successful completion of the project. It is always a good idea to start collaborations with short, simple projects to build trust, work out communication, and iron out the kinks in task sharing.

Organize carefully. Consider details in the beginning before hands are shaken or agreements are signed. Draft an "e-mail of understanding" about what is involved in the collaboration, including the expected outcomes, stated in the most specific way possible. Agree to a timeline that includes mutually-accepted deadlines for major phases or the project as a whole.

> The most important element in success is for the collaborating institutions to be clear on what they need from each other, and on what they have to offer in return.

Library partnerships succeed when there is good planning, where resources are adequate, when communication is regular, when project managers are responsible for managing the success of the joint venture, and when the partners view themselves as stakeholders.

From the moment of a collaboration's inception, the person managing the partnership's success must be conscious of evaluation. Evaluation discussions and measurement systems should be established where needed, and with outside evaluators employed if appropriate. If the partnership is with an agency or organization that does "not want to bother with evaluation," the appropriate comment is, "How will we measure our success?" Partnerships have a way of producing serendipitous outcomes – which are fine, so long as desired outcomes are achieved as well. An example might be a school-church-library partnership to get 500 more kids to read in aftercare. Lots of good outcomes may flow from this project, such as a television editorial about how good it is to see organizations cooperating to help children read. Teachers are happy because the public library is offering "book bags" and "book boxes" for use in after care classrooms, and the library sees its card registration skyrocket. Unless measured change in aftercare reading participation occurs, however, the positive outcomes are serendipitous.

Partnerships can play a significant role in helping libraries accomplish their missions. Collaborative activities are not appropriate for all organizations, at the same time or in the same way. Library leaders will recognize that different cultural conditions and different operating circumstances create variant partnership needs and opportunities for different libraries. With partnerships, as with all other library policy strategies, differences between libraries are as significant as the similarities that join them. Collaboration is a wonderful tool, one that can help a library achieve its mission-driven outcomes within the rhythms of its institutional life. And, the outcome of successful partnerships makes those who are served by them the big winners.

Pierce College Library, operating at its two campuses at Lakewood and Puyallup, WA, partnered with its faculty members to integrate library resources and skills instruction into subject classes. Together, the groups developed Information Competency Skills library courses that made students more successful in their classes.

Like Pierce, the Libraries at the University of Texas at Arlington built a partnership relationship with faculty setting them up to offer valuable, high interest programs in an informal, collegial setting. The programs featured accomplished faculty members, built relationships with them, improved the library's reputation as a proactive campus institution and brought students quality information they did not have previously.

Tucson-Pima (AZ) Public Library partnered with its teen users, giving them a strong voice in library programming, hiring and training some to help other teens be successful. The teen partners also help full-time staff deliver teen services more effectively.

Wauconda Area (IL) Public Library partnered with local businesses in implementing the PLA's "Smartest Card" campaign to offer free merchandise and discounts to customers who presented their cards at the time of purchase. The campaign resulted in the issuance of hundreds of new library cards, created a high-visibility community celebration for "Library Card Sign-up Month," and tightened the library's relationship with area merchants.

Williamsburg (VA) Regional Library used partnering as a strategic tool to accomplish its mission. The effort resulted in new and important outcome links to a hospital, school and non-profit businesses. These examples are just a sampling of the myriad partnership and collaboration opportunities today's effective libraries can consider.

Collaboration is a wonderful tool, one that can help a library achieve its mission-driven outcomes within the rhythms of its institutional life.

CASE STUDY: UNIVERSITY OF TEXAS AT ARLINGTON, ARLINGTON, TX

"We try not to think of ourselves as just the library,
but as part of the campus and the community.
We look for projects we can do with other departments."

Tommie Wingfield
Assistant to the Directorate for Marketing & External Relations
University of Texas at Arlington

Challenges

- Deepen collaboration between Library staff and faculty in other departments

- Highlight the exceptional caliber of UT-Arlington faculty, with no extra funding

Solutions

- "Focus on Faculty" speaker series, and other programs

- Partner with university departments to offer unique and valuable student programs

- Tap university publicity office to design & disseminate advertising materials

Benefits

- Building strong relationships with influential faculty

- Promoting faculty achievements to the university community

- Improving Library's reputation as an asset with a variety of services

- Securing positive publicity within existing budget

OVERVIEW

The University of Texas at Arlington (UTA) has over 25,000 students, more than 5,000 staff and faculty, and three libraries with a collection of approximately 1 million volumes. The libraries are known collectively as one organization called the UTA Libraries. Taking an active role in campus collaboration, the UTA Libraries' staff co-sponsors a variety of programs aimed at building student awareness of the high-caliber university faculty research and expertise.

Among the multifaceted initiatives is the "Focus on Faculty" speaker series. Launched in 2002, it features UTA faculty members and their award-winning research, ranging across varied fields of study. Sponsoring this series has helped the UTA Libraries organization make strides in building relationships among students and faculty alike. Faculty members enjoy greater visibility and recognition for their achievements, both on campus and in the community. Tommie Wingfield, assistant to the directorate for marketing and external relations captures the essence of the Libraries' mission, saying, "We try not to think of ourselves as just the library, but as part of the campus and the community. We look for projects we can do with other departments."

CHALLENGE

The UTA Libraries wanted to deepen collaboration with other academic departments, and boost student awareness of resources and faculty expertise on their academic doorstep. Several years ago, the Libraries' faculty recognized that student awareness was low, and were determined to work with other departments to formulate programs involving the entire campus population.

SOLUTION

The basic premise behind each collaborative initiative is to focus on the scholarship and expertise within departments, capitalize on the UTA Libraries' skill and strength as an information resource, and then share it with the campus community. Organization and advance publicity are integral for the programs' ongoing success.

For example, the "Focus on Faculty" speaker series hosts six programs during the academic year, between September and April. They are open to the campus and the wider Arlington communities. To make a splash, organizers prepare a campus publicity campaign to promote the speakers, one that could serve as a model for others.

Wingfield turns to UTA's own publicity office to design and disseminate advertising materials, thus keeping expenses down. "Our base funding never changed, so we maximize our existing resources to launch our collaborative programs. It is logical to tap internal expertise," she says.

First, Wingfield, Libraries faculty, and publicity office specialists choose the materials to be included:

- Posters, banners, postcards, library newsletters, press releases and invitations
- University and library website promotions, LCD monitors in libraries, electronic calendars, and electronic listservs
- Postings on the campus and free student newspaper calendars, and bulletin boards

They plan to have materials ready for display three weeks prior to each presentation, meeting with all faculty departments and offices involved to secure permissions and establish lead times for completion. The To Do list includes the following:

- Select speakers from a "shopping list" – UTA's list of faculty awards, Faculty named to the Academy of Distinguished Scholars, New deans, Topic experts.
  Lead time: one to two years
- Meet with library web managers to publicize events on the site.
  Lead time: six weeks
- Negotiate design and printing costs for a single template design.
  Cost for monthly customized edits
  Costs for Postcard/banner/poster color printing
  Lead time: five to six weeks
- Discuss design work with the Publicity Office.
- Request permission from campus Student Activities and Student Government groups to post materials and send information to related sponsors via internal listservs.
- Reserve meeting rooms, equipment, refreshments; prepare faculty introductions and handouts, speaker gifts, and event welcome details.

BENEFITS

For UTA Libraries, the benefits have been sizeable. It has forged strong relationships with students and influential faculty members. It has publicized faculty accomplishments to the university community, http://library.uta.edu/newsEvents/. Other departments contribute to the Libraries' influence through collaborative campus relationships. For example, the Information Literacy and Information Services departments team with Student Affairs to celebrate Academic Integrity Week without taxing budgets. The reaction to these offerings has been huge. According to Wingfield, "The faculty loves it, and sees the library as a friendly, collegial place."

In September 2005, the Libraries and the Department of Physics jointly funded and sponsored campus celebrations of the Einstein Centennial as part of the World Year of Physics 2005. Events combined "Focus on Faculty" with programs featuring a physicist of international stature. It was an appropriate forum, as the UTA Libraries proves that necessity overcomes inertia, and generates creative action.

Figure 1.
Excerpt from UTA
"Focus on Faculty" publicity poster

CASE STUDY: PIERCE COLLEGE, LAKEWOOD, WA AND PUYALLUP, WA

"Our approach to teaching integrated library coursework is to exist in other classes, like a business course or an English course. It's the point of need instruction with the bigger picture in mind."

Lynn Olson
Reference and Instruction Librarian
Pierce College

Challenges

• Integrate the Library resources into the school and the community

• Help students learn the tools and skills they will need for future education or the job market

Solutions

• Formed the Information Competency Program to teach library courses that change each year depending on the needs of students and faculty

• Work with faculty to have classes integrate teaching of library resources and skills

• Provide students research skills through library courses

• Incorporate class and library-developed assignments that teach research and writing skills

• Listen, attend and respond to needs of faculty and students

Benefits

• Created strong ties between the Library and college administrators, faculty, and students

• Students get to know library staff and see them as advisors and key resources

• Many students transfer to the University of Washington with positive results

• According to Pierce faculty, the work students produce after attending a library integrated course is much stronger

Overview

Pierce College is a community college serving as a bridge for students, either to another university or to the work force. From its campuses in Lakewood and Puyallup, Washington, Pierce builds student skills in the college's Five Core Abilities. Critical Thinking and Problem Solving, Effective Communication, Information Competency, Multiculturalism, and Responsibility are the heart of the academic curriculum.

To integrate library concepts, abilities, skills, and resources into the core curriculum areas, library faculty and school administrators worked together to create and teach an offering of integrated study, known as The Information Competency Program. In 2005, the program attracted the attention of the Association of College Research and Research Librarians (ACRL). It awarded Pierce College the Excellence in Academic Libraries Award, for being a national community college leader in student outcomes assessment.

Challenges

The Information Competency Program developed from goals to stress the importance of academic research skills and promote the Library as a vital student support center. The Library faculty wanted to help students see the library not only as a place to do research, but also as a support center with a friendly, knowledgeable staff dedicated to helping them succeed in their diverse pursuits. With no students living on either campus, the Library wanted to be a place where students, subject area faculty, and library staff could feel connected, and comfortable using resources. Each student group – recent high school graduates, international students, second-year students, both full and part time – had specific and varied educational needs, and the Library wanted to be able to help address them.

Solutions

To meet the varied instructional needs of the college's students, library professional staff decided several years ago to shift the organization's focus from service to teaching. That meant finding ways to involve library faculty in subject course instruction. The solution became coordinated library instructional offerings known as "linked classes." Together, the classes formed The Information Competency Program. The program integrates critical thinking and evaluation into the disciplinary content of these classes, in a way that not only helps leverage course material but also helps students hone skills such as conducting online research or writing research papers. "Our approach to teaching integrated coursework," explains Lynn Olson, a reference and instruction librarian, "is to exist in other classes like a business course or an English course. It's the point of need instruction with the bigger picture in mind."

Dean of Libraries Debra Gilchrist explains that the courses have evolved over the years to "teach more in an outcome-based mode." She adds, "What's important is that this is now a college initiative, not just a library initiative." One of the most important integrated classes is English 101, an entry-level English course that integrates research and technology. It is also considered a threshold course, one that will either keep or deter students. "If students do well," explains Olson, "we'll retain them. If not, they'll leave school. So we're trying to make an impact here. It's a high goal."

Each year, the seven full-time and four part-time librarians meet with the other Pierce faculty and decide which classes will be taught with the Information Competency Program. Though integrated classes change each year, the material and tools presented remain the same. Reference and Information Librarian Christie Flynn says, "All of the faculty know that students need these skills, whether it's the English student who transfers to a university after two years at Pierce, or the student who wants to be the front office manager of a medical building after graduating."

The linked classes are offered once or up to several times a week, and meet from two to six hours at a time, depending on the nature of the curriculum and the target student audience. Some of the subjects librarians cover include: effective research in the library and online, finding and citing quotes from books, and using and evaluating online databases. Any student may enroll; and some faculty members now require their students to attend linked classes. Flynn stresses that teaching students about the online databases is especially important, because the library is not always open and has limited hours during the summer. "Students need to know they can do research using the Library's databases even when they are not in the Library."

Other subjects that are consistently part of the Information Competency Program are history, sociology, and business. Classes address current problems in academia, such as plagiarism, and instructors develop specific assignments to instruct students on avoiding missteps. Christie Flynn also offers a stand-alone, two-credit, 20-hour class on library research methods. "It works because it's in the context of a learning community," she explains. "This course is very popular with the social services majors, especially the mental health class Pierce offers." Olsen confirms, "The library is a classroom."

BENEFITS

Though Pierce has not yet engaged formal methods to gather feedback on the linked classes or specifically on the Information Competency Program, word of mouth from current and former students assures them that these classes are working. Students value the ability they have to apply their skills in their daily life. Olson says that students are definitely using online resources more because of the classes. "When things go down on the Library web page," she explains, "and I'm trying to fix it, I get calls from students about where the problems are. Students go out and use the resources, and value them." College department chairs also report that students involved in the program produce higher caliber work. They see evidence of student learning. They use a variety of assessment tools and continue to revise them in order to get at the heart of what their contribution is to the student body.

The Library is now more connected to the rest of the Pierce College community. Students can choose a librarian to be their academic advisor, and they now see library faculty members as valuable resources not only at the library, but for their college careers. The initiative also promotes collaboration between the Library and subject discipline faculties. "We try not to live in the library itself," Olson says. "When there's a new faculty orientation, we're there talking about the Information Competency Program." In this way, the subject faculty uses the same resources students will tap for their course work.

The Pierce librarians and faculty are now working to improve and extend the Information Competency Program to include more classes, and are considering a capstone project for which students apply all of the research skills they've learned into one final project. This assignment would validate that students are applying program skills to their academic work.

"Partnering is a strategic tool that flows from the library's mission and vision, embracing a library-wide strategy. It relies on a formal adoption process and central coordination for success."

Janet Crowther
Outreach Services Director
Williamsburg Regional Library

Challenges

- Make the Library a participant in many different kinds of partnerships

- Define library partnership as it applies to their organization

- Formalize partnership structures and procedures to best suit

Solutions

- Establish formal guidelines for partnership

- Approach partnership as a strategic tool

- View partnerships as you would human relationships to determine level of involvement and duration of the partnership

- Educate staff across departments in partnership procedures and management

Benefits

- Hospital partnership yielded funding and expertise to develop an award-winning cancer resource center at the Library

- Nonprofit business partnership forged important link to the nonprofit business community and resources

- School partnership survey program increased Library visibility among school administrators, students and teachers

OVERVIEW

The Williamsburg Regional Library is part of a regional system serving 60,000 people through two branches and one mobile services vehicle. It is funded by both city and county governments. In 2000, the Library adopted a formula for successful library partnerships founded on definitions that mirror human relationships. Potential partners are designated as "glances, dates, engagements, and marriages," depending on their ability to help the Library pursue its mission. Employing the formula and guidelines described below, the Library maintains 16 thriving community "marriages."

Challenge - Opportunity Knocks

In 1999, the Sentara Williamsburg (VA) Community Hospital contacted Williamsburg Regional Library Outreach Services Director Janet Crowther proposing the creation of a cancer resource center at the Library. The proposal represented a symbiotic collaboration in which the hospital would provide a level of funding and marketing for the creation of a medical information resource center that the Library would not have been able to commit on its own. In turn, the Library would provide the space and staff skills for expanding public access to important consumer health information.

Crowther came away from the call intent on founding the project. "From that contact came a moment when we all recognized the potential for the library to be a broad-based contact for partnerships that work with our mission," she says. Between 1999 and 2000, Crowther teamed with Adult Services Director Barry Trott, the library director, and department managers to form the Library's Community Partnership Development Group. This team researched and codified formal structures and procedures to guide the development of partnerships that would best serve the Library's mission.

Solution

In 1999, the Library inaugurated the Philip West Memorial Cancer Resource Center, named for a local resident whose bequest helped found the center. Through mid-2006, the hospital has committed $16,000 in advertising dollars to promote use of the center, and a total of $50,000 to fund the resources. The hospital also fully funds and conducts four Cancer Resource Center programs yearly at the library.
The Library provides the center's physical space and professional skills, such as cataloging, administration, and overall resource integration and delivery. The center maintains a website and provides access to a wide range of local and global cancer resources for patients, their families, and caregivers. Resources include e-books, brochures, web links to discussion groups, physicians, support and advocacy groups, and access to health and wellness databases.[1] Crowther comments on the importance of testing any partnership proposal against the litmus of the mission, "Most of the time, when librarians talk about partnerships, they're talking about a single event – usually one where the library is doing most of the work. With too many libraries, it's about the library giving and not receiving." Trott adds to this an important caveat, "You should never look at partnerships as a substitute for funding. It's not going to solve your funding problems or other library problems."

Instead, libraries should view partnering as a strategic tool. Crowther and Trott propose a unique definition of partnering to guide library strategic planning. This concept is detailed in their published work, *Partnering with Purpose: a Guide to Strategic Partnership Development for Libraries and other Organizations* (by Crowther, J., and Trott, B., Libraries Unlimited, 2004).

Partnering Is a Strategic Tool
- It flows out of the library's mission and vision
- It's a library-wide strategy
- It is centrally coordinated
- It is a formal process[2]

Partnering is also scalable. Big or small, a library that can bring something to the table has the potential to collaborate for the benefit of both partners. And how do you know if opportunity is truly knocking?

Definition of Partnership

The Williamsburg Regional Library experience indicates that all library decision makers must share a clear operating definition of what partnership is, and the ability to judge a proposal's merit. To acknowledge the importance of all library-community relationships, but to differentiate between the levels of library-partner involvement, the Williamsburg Regional Library has defined the term "partnership" in the context of a human relations analogy. It includes four types of relationships: glances, dates, engagements, and marriages.

Glance: any overture or contact between the library and a community group.

Date: an agreement between the library and a community partner to accomplish a specific short-term activity or commitment.

Engagement: an agreement between the library and a community partner to work together toward a marriage after an initial experimental phase. Engagements are temporal; they either evolve into a marriage, dissolve, or downsize to a date.

Marriage: a formal agreement between the library and a community partner with compatible goals, to share the work, share the risk, and share the results or proceeds. The library and the community partner jointly invest in resources, experience mutual benefits, and share risk, responsibility, authority, and accountability. Marriages are formed for the long-term benefit to the partners. [3]

The Community Partnership Development Group reviews all engagement or marriage-level partnership possibilities, and selects those appropriate to pursue. Says Crowther, "We think about what's important to the community and how the Library needs to respond. We field suggestions and vet them through the group." Members meet formally three times per year, and in addition to Crowther and Trott, members include the library director, the development director, the assistant director, and public services division heads. The community services librarian and other library staff also keep an eye out for partnering opportunities.

Williamsburg: Steps in Choosing a Partner

1. Know what you want to achieve for your library through partnering and why.
2. Troll the community and make a short list of potential partners.
3. Guide your partner selection based on the following:
   - What is the partner's mission and does it complement the library's mission?
   - What is the partner's position in the community?
   - Who are the groups or segments of the community served by the partner?
   - What sort of resources – assets and strengths – might this partnership bring to the relationship and project goals?
   - What are the partner's strategic directions?
   - Who are the leaders in this organization?
   - Does the timing seem right?
   - What is the partner's corporate culture and can you work together?
   - Is the partner's planning and budget cycle one you can work with?
   - Are unique opportunities arising? [4]

Accepted Williamsburg partners sign a formal Partnership Agreement, "...a letter of understanding between the parties to state the goals of the partnership and to enumerate the project responsibilities for each party." [5]

Potential Partners
Businesses
Civic Groups
Nonprofit organizations including museums – local, state, national
Schools and colleges
Libraries of all types
Government agencies – local, state, federal[6]

Reasons to Use the Partnership Tool
Reach new library users
Reach current library patrons in a new way
Tap into community assets and strengths
Gain support for library resources/programs
Gain valuable feedback
Create new library resources[7]

Managing Partnerships
Williamsburg Regional Library's established partnerships are supervised by the Library's community services manager, and 12 different people with different staff roles, from department heads to assistants. "The structure of our program helps us manage partnerships that couldn't otherwise exist. Without structure, you can't track your partnership, you can't resolve problems, and no one can receive credit for what's being achieved," says Trott.

The Library's various partnership managers maintain ongoing discussion with partners throughout the year, culminating with delivery of a two-part evaluation form in which both the Library and the partner reflect on the past year. Both parties note any adjustments or new directions they believe the partnership should take.

BENEFITS – SOME EXAMPLES

The Williamsburg Community Health Foundation Partnership.
- $50,000 in total funding for a grant writing collection housed at the Library.
- Hosting a growing local nonprofit listserv of 50 current members.
- Library recognition from the business community as a focal point for nonprofit business training and discussion. Four funded workshops take place at the Library each year.
- An important link to the nonprofit business community and its resources.

Figure 1.

The Phillip West Memorial Cancer Resource Center Partnership

- $50,000 in total Library funding from the hospital
- $16,000 in advertising dollars spent by the hospital to promote the center
- $35,000 endowment given to the Williamsburg Regional Library Foundation to support center programming. The endowment was made by a grateful cancer patient who had made use of center resources
- Four hospital-funded cancer center programs held at the Library each year
- Cancer Resource Center Awards include the Virginia Library Association George Mason Award, 1999, for distinguished advocacy of libraries, providing local and national information on cancer that would not otherwise have been available to the public.

The Williamsburg-James City County Public Schools Partnership

- Yearly Library access to 9,500 students, and 1,100 teachers/staff for important survey feedback regarding their use of library services and their preferences for public library programming.
- New teacher library luncheons – The Library offers one-hour presentations and resource packages about library services to all incoming teachers.
- The Library/school survey was effective most importantly because it received the endorsement of all the principals. High-level approval from such offices as principal and superintendent often improves the chances of program acceptance in a school. In Williamsburg's case, it yielded some 3,500 survey returns. "Our stature has increased locally because of our partnership with the schools," say Trott. "The Library's work in the schools is more directly recognized by county and city administrators."

Along with these specific outcomes, the Williamsburg Library's approach to partnerships has yielded overall benefits as well. The partnership formula added useful structure to the organization's decision making, for example, making space request decisions easier. Partnerships have also helped give the Library a deeper understanding of neighborhood connections, and higher visibility among funding policy makers.

The Williamsburg experience also demonstrates that even seemingly unequal partnerships can be effective. For many years the Library has partnered with AARP to offer free tax services at the Library, including electronic tax return filing. Crowther notes that at first glance the AARP tax service might be seen as something of an "unbalanced partnership" not offering much benefit to the Library. Taking a longer view, she says that allowing AARP to offer the service on Library premises gives seniors another reason to see the Library as a community agency that provides important services to them.

Crowther says the partnering program reflects the Library's organizational style. "It's gratifying to see everyone on the same page," she says. "At Williamsburg Regional Library, the strategic partnering program has evolved into an accepted, valued practice. This institution has embraced it and has allowed the process to work."

Trott comments on the internal benefits that partnerships bring to the Library. "It's been rewarding to work with a Library to achieve things, working across departments. The interdepartmental cooperation has really made partnering possible. It's gratifying to gather in a public library with library and community professionals to talk about something new."

Suggested Reading

Crowther, Janet H., and Barry Trott, *Partnering with Purpose: A Guide to Strategic Partnership Development for Libraries and Other Organizations* (Westport, CT: Libraries Unlimited, 2004).

Endnotes

[1] Phillip West Memorial Cancer Resource Center, <http://www.westcancer.org/index/index.html>.

[2] Janet H. Crowther and Barry Trott, "Guidelines for Developing Community Partnerships," *Partnering with a Purpose: A Guide to Strategic Partnership Development for Libraries and Other Organizations* (Westport, CT: Libraries Unlimited, 2004).

[3] Ibid.

[4] Ibid.

[5] *Williamsburg Regional Library Partnership Agreement* (August 2005) paragraph 1.

[6] Janet H. Crowther and Barry Trott, "Guidelines for Developing Community Partnerships," *Partnering with a Purpose: A Guide to Strategic Partnership Development for Libraries and Other Organizations* (Westport, CT: Libraries Unlimited, 2004).

[7] Ibid.

"The basic premise of the Smartest Card was that the library is here to serve the community. It is one thing to own a library card; it's another thing to use it."

Kathy Nielsen
Circulation Manager
Wauconda Area Library

Challenges

- Heighten awareness of the value of a library card

- Increase the library's identity within the community

- Support local small businesses

Solutions

- Partner with local businesses to offer discounts and free merchandise when customers present their library card

- Implement PLA's Library Card Sign Up campaign, the "Smartest Card," to plan an annual local promotion

- Create a community celebration for "Library Card Sign-Up Month"

Benefits

- During September 2005, 531 new patrons registered for library cards; hundreds more received replacement cards or keychain cards

- Library has a renewed identity and increased visibility within the community

- Library recognized by consortium as "Library of the Year"

OVERVIEW

As a public library serving a variety of users, the Wauconda Area Library has always looked for ways to increase library patronage and partner with the community. Wauconda library staff started working with local small businesses to create a library card partnership program in 1999. The initiative promoted library card enrollment by offering discounts and free gifts through local businesses. In 2004, the library incorporated the Public Library Association's "Smartest Card" concept into its library card promotional campaign. The number of participating businesses has grown from 22 in 1999 to 126 in 2006. This successful community outreach program has dramatically increased the number of library cardholders, strengthened relations between the Library and the business community, and garnered deserved recognition for the Wauconda Area Library staff.

CHALLENGE

Located in the far northwest suburbs of Chicago, the Wauconda Area Public Library District serves six villages with a total population of approximately 24,000 residents. The Library has historically had a strong outreach program, participating in various community events, and working closely with the school district and community organizations. Focus, the Library's print newsletter, is mailed to every home and business in the library district four times a year, promoting new services and a variety of exciting activities such as focused reading clubs, teen anime clubs, concerts, movies, and computer classes, all designed to draw patrons to the Library.

Still, the Wauconda staff always looks for new opportunities. According to library Circulation Manager Kathy Nielsen, "The Library's circulation goals are twofold: 1) to reach out to people who don't have a library card, and, 2) to encourage those that have library cards to use them! We are always looking for new ways to increase our patronage."

After hearing then General Colin Powell's 1999 ALA keynote address, and reading through some of the related materials made available afterwards, Nielsen was inspired. She formulated an idea to expand the Library's role within the library district by tapping the local business community to help encourage library card enrollment.

SOLUTIONS

From its inauguration in 1999, the program's template for success has been simple. Each September (National Library Card Sign-Up Month), participating businesses offer free products or discounts to customers who present their library card. Examples include two-for-one admission to a museum, 10 percent discounts on auto repair, or a free drink with the purchase of a sandwich.

The campaign runs throughout the month of September, but planning continues throughout the year as library staff make appearances at local business expos and community events. Library staff works with the local Chamber of Commerce at the annual Business Expo and this helps to identify new businesses and prospective business partners.

Taking their cues from the PLA "Smartest Card" Campaign Toolkit, Wauconda staff have created a variety of marketing materials, including brochures, newsletter articles, press releases, and posters. They create a customized window sign for each business that takes part in the program. "It's so cool," Nielsen remarks, "to drive around the library district and see those special signs hanging in the storefront windows during the month of September."

To further reinforce the value of the program, the Library distributes a flyer listing the participating businesses and their specific promotions. The information is also listed on the Library website, with links to each business address, telephone number, and website. The Wauconda team also attracts patrons by offering prizes and giveaways at the Library. Book store gift cards are only some of the 30 recent raffle prizes awarded to patrons who used their Wauconda Area Library card during the month of September.

BENEFITS

Wauconda Area Library's Library Card Partnership is a winning proposition for everyone. By publicizing the discount program, the Library gains new patrons, patronage at local businesses is promoted, and residents receive a free or discounted item or service. "Businesses now value this opportunity to partner with the library," reports Tom Kern, the Library's director. "They receive the benefit of free advertising through our newsletter, flyers, our e-News and website, and the advertisements we post on the local cable network."

The growth of the program is testament to its success: 22 businesses participated in the initial Library Card partnership in 1999. By 2005, there were 120 businesses participating, as well as 130 individual McDonald's franchises across central to northern Illinois. "Now businesses approach us and call about getting involved," says Nielsen. After all is said and done, this district-wide annual promotion very effectively serves the Library's objectives to heighten public awareness of the value of having a library card.

Success is not limited to business involvement and new cardholders. Since the promotion began, the Wauconda Area Library circulation has risen substantially each year, from a total circulation of about 330,000 in 1999 to 543,000 in 2006 – a growth of about 65 percent. Additionally, library program attendance and other aspects of library usage have increased at the same healthy rate. In September 2005, 531 new patrons registered for library cards; hundreds more received replacement cards or key chain cards. As Nielsen points out, "Our initiative's basic premise is that the library is here to serve the community. It is one thing to own a library card; it's another thing to use it."

Finally, to cap off the benefits of its creative outreach efforts, the Wauconda Area Library was named "Library of the Year" in 2005 by the North Suburban Library System, a consortium of 650 academic, public, school and special libraries in north suburban Cook, Kane, Lake and McHenry counties. The award will only motivate this library's dedicated staff to stay attuned to patron needs and seek new opportunities and partners.

Figure 1.
Focus – Library Newsletter

Figure 2.
Wauconda Area Library Website –
Library Partnership Web Page

"Because of this partnership initiative, we now have a greater understanding of what youth development is. We realize that offering a single program now and then, as we once did, won't help teens achieve long-term goals. The initiative has led to stronger relationships between teens & librarians and with evaluation tools from the the Public Libraries as Partners in Youth Development Initiative (PLPYD), we know that we have had a significant impact on the lives of teens in the program."

Gina Macaluso
Coordinator of Youth Services
Tucson-Pima Public Library

Challenges

- Secure grants to develop long-term educational and career development programs for teens

- Communicate directly with area teens to learn their needs

- Give teens more of a voice in library programming that affects them

- Create a welcoming library environment for teens

Solutions

- Awarded planning and implementation grants from the Wallace Foundation

- Attended extensive staff training sessions in youth development principles

- Conducted extensive surveys of area teens and library staff

- Created paid employment opportunities for teens

  - teen computer aide

  - youth advisory council

  - teen advocates

Benefits

- Training and metrics give library staff a new understanding of youth development principles, and a deeper capacity to create programs to serve teens; help staff know they are successful

- Training and close working relationships change staff and teen attitudes and improve ability to assist each other

- Teen employee skills increase the library's service to constituents

OVERVIEW

Funded by the City of Tucson and Pima County, Arizona, the Tucson-Pima Public Library serves approximately 700,000 visitors per year in several low-income communities across its 25 branches. In 1999, the library joined nine public libraries across the country to participate in the Public Libraries as Partners in Youth Development Initiative (PLPYD). This four-year grant initiative is sponsored by the Wallace Foundation (wallacefunds.org), which "seeks to support and share effective ideas and practices that will strengthen education leadership, arts participation and out-of-school learning."[1]

Invited to employ grant monies to "develop or expand youth programs that engaged individual teens in a developmentally supportive manner, while enhancing library services for all youth in the community," the libraries were "encouraged to ground their work in youth development principles, and to develop partnerships with schools and other community institutions."[2] The first grant award of $30,000 funded a year of strategic analysis and planning. The second grant, totaling $400,000 covered program implementation over three years.

The Library developed planning and implementation strategies in partnership with teens through local schools, community colleges, government institutions and youth services organizations. Using PLPYD metrics, library staff assessed its teen education enrichment and career services initiatives.

Key Findings:

- Professional training is an important factor in creating and fostering an environment that promotes long-term youth development.

- Teens will develop and contribute to library programs if given an active role and incentives for long-term teen employment.

CHALLENGES

Reaching out to teen constituents

Historically, the Tucson-Pima Public Library has sponsored teen-centered library services in the community, as Youth Services Coordinator Gina Macaluso points out. "We were already doing work beyond our local branches. Our homework help tutoring program was an established service for the community," she explains. However, other programs for teens were limited, one-time offerings, such as SAT classes and writing workshops. "Like many libraries at the time, teens were often viewed as the step-children of the library world," she adds, "and we wanted to be more in tune with their needs, and strengthen our services for youth."

The Wallace initiative's objective to "support the development of innovative models for public library systems to provide high quality educational enrichment and career development programs for underserved low-income teenagers and children..." provided an ideal opportunity to act. [3]

SOLUTIONS – PLANNING

During the first grant year, Macaluso coordinated two library task forces comprised of library staff members and youth advisors to assess internal and external library practices for their effectiveness in promoting youth development. Both teams worked closely with the local high schools, community college, the juvenile detention center and the Arizona education advocacy group, Metropolitan Education Commission, to identify youth services agencies in the area and help recruit teens for their feedback.

The task forces conducted extensive surveys and convened several focus groups of youths, parents and local youth service providers. Focus groups were comprised of 10 participants, with youth and parents interviewed separately from staff. Questions related to personal interaction with the Library – experience with library services, overall satisfaction, access to library branches and services – with the aim of assessing library strengths and weaknesses in teen programming (Figure 1).

With guidance from the PLPYD administrators, Macaluso and her colleagues analyzed survey results. Responses helped her get to the heart of key questions. Why do we want teens in the Library? What is our library mission in this regard? If we want to help teens develop and become literate, contributing members of society, what education and employment agendas can this Library implement to meet that goal? What do teens want from the Library? What ideas are they giving us through the survey process?

Items to Implement

Armed with answers, Library staff drafted an implementation grant proposal that would initiate professional training to make the entire library system more effective in working with teen users, and incorporating their suggestions for library programming and communication over the next three years. The proposal contained the following provisions.

Create a friendly, welcoming environment for teens

Professional Development Training:
Tucson-Pima staff participated in extensive training sponsored by the Wallace Foundation to deepen their understanding of youth development principles. "We did a great deal of training for our staff, attending monthly presentations learning about positive youth development, youth at risk, and adolescent cognitive development," notes Macaluso.

Combined with survey data, the library training led to the creation of a teen advisory group whose members would act as liaisons between the Library and youths, helping to fashion and revise library programming geared to that audience. Branch librarians worked directly with their school counterparts in the area to establish the group and attract members.

Provide incentives for long-term teen employment, to encourage teen contribution to library programs:
The Library created employment opportunities in two areas to mutually benefit area teens and the Library – computer services and advocacy. Teens were hired and trained as library computer aides to assist patron computer-related research. The work offered teens paid employment, academic credit, and freed up Library staff for other Library priorities.

The Teen Advocates received stipends for their service as library advocates. They communicate library services to the Friends of the Library committee, their peers in school, other youth services organizations, and also recruit other teens to participate in programs. All advocates make annual presentations to five area organizations.

Benefits

The efforts yielded significant beneficial changes in attitude and library practices. They dispelled many false assumptions each group had framed about the other. As a result, staff and teens have become more comfortable interacting directly with each other. It's now common for library personnel to step out from behind a desk to work with teen patrons, to ask directly for their opinions or concerns. Teens also interact differently, now that their presence is no longer anonymous. They feel valued and are more willing to influence the behavior of their peers while in the library. These findings echo the PLPYD Initiative's overall conclusions:

- Training and close working relationships change staff attitudes toward youths and improve the ability to assist them. Talk to teens, ask them what they want, learn their names, involve them.
- Training and close working relationships can change teen attitudes toward library staff and create incentives for long-term teen employment.
- Teens are resources that deepen and broaden the Tucson-Pima Public Library's capacity to serve its constituents.
- Teens value their role as library contributors, aides, and advocates.
- Teens can effectively communicate their library experience to peer groups and community organizations.
- Library staff gained a new understanding of the meaning of youth development principles, and a deeper capacity to create programs to serve teens.[4]

Gina Macaluso points out that the teen computer aide program was her Library's most successful effort. It remains a paying opportunity, and has increased the Library's capacity to serve its constituency. All library patrons benefit from the assistance and knowledge the aides provide. The aides themselves have acquired new job skills in a mentoring environment, which builds a foundation for the future. The Teen Advocacy program also continues, and boasts 15 teen advocates.

"Because of the PLPYD Initiative, we now have a greater understanding of what youth development is. We realize now that offering a single program now and then, as we once did, won't help teens achieve long-term goals. The initiative has led to stronger relationships between teens & librarians, and with strong evaluation mechanisms, we know that we have had a significant impact on the lives of teens in the program."

RECOMMENDED READING

Gnehm, Kurstin Finch, ed. *Youth Development and Public Libraries*. Urban Libraries Council, 2002.

ENDNOTES

[1] *The Wallace Foundation*, <http://www.wallacefoundation.org/WF/>.

[2] Julie Spielberger, Carol Horton and Lisa Michels, *New on the Shelf: Teens in the Library: Summary of Key Findings from the Evaluation of Public Libraries as Partners in Youth Development*, A Wallace Foundation Initiative (Chicago: University of Chicago, 2004) 2.

[3] Ibid.

[4] Ibid, pg 3.

Figure 1. Survey Sample 1

TUCSON-PIMA PUBLIC LIBRARY
PUBLIC LIBRARIES AS PARTNERS IN YOUTH DEVELOPMENT SURVEY

1. What grade are you in school? (circle one)
   ☐ 5th ☐ 6th ☐ 7th ☐ 8th ☐ 9th ☐ 10th ☐ 11th ☐ 12th ☐ Other

2. Which school do you attend? _____

3. Check one: ☐ Male ☐ Female

4. Do you have a Tucson-Pima Public Library card? ☐ Yes ☐ No

5. How do you get from place to place: ☐ Walk ☐ Bike ☐ Bus pass ☐ Car ☐ Parent
   ☐ Other _____

EDUCATIONAL ENRICHMENT:

Opportunities to learn more about the world so teens can find their place in it.

1. Outside of the classroom, which of these do you use most for information to help you with school? (circle your top five)
   Teachers   Guidance counselors   School activities   School Library Friends   Parent or Relative
   Computers/Internet   Magazines   Radio   Clubs or Organizations   Adult or Mentor
   Public Library   Other_____

2. Have you used a public library in the past year to help with schoolwork? ☐ Yes ☐ No
   If yes, circle all of those that apply.
   Went to library   Called the library   Website   Visited with my class
   Librarian was at a program I went to in the community   Used Homework Help program
   Other _____

3. When you use the library, do you find what you need? ☐ Yes ☐ No
   Why or why not: _____
   _____

4. Do you have access to computers and the Internet for schoolwork? ☐ Yes ☐ No ☐ Not enough

5. Would you like more training or information about how to use computers? ☐ Yes ☐ No

6. For you, which is the most important reason for getting a good education?
   ☐ Getting a good job ☐ Opportunity to learn new things ☐ Knowing technology
   ☐ Discovering what I am good at ☐ Learning life skills ☐ Other _____

7. What are your educational plans?
   ☐ High School/GED ☐ 2 yr (for example, Pima College) ☐ Trade school (for example, ITT Tech)
   ☐ College/university (for example, University of Arizona) ☐ Enlist in Military

8. How important will the public library be to you after you finish school?
   ☐ Not at all ☐ Somewhat useful ☐ I'll use it if I need to ☐ I will use it regularly

continued on next page

CAREER DEVELOPMENT:

Opportunities to learn more about careers and work.

1. Are you working after school? ☐ Yes   ☐ No

2. Do you work during the summer? ☐ Yes   ☐ No

3. Do you get paid for working? ☐ Yes   ☐ No

4. Do you do volunteer work? ☐ Yes   ☐ No

5. Was it difficult for you to find a job? ☐ Yes   ☐ No

6. How did you find your job? _____

7. Where do you work? _____

8. Who do you talk to about planning your career? (Mark 1st, 2nd & 3rd choice)
   Self___ Family___ Friends___ Librarian ___ School Counselor___ Adult you respect___
   Someone working in that job___ Other_____

9. Where would you look for information about careers? (Mark 1st, 2nd, 3rd choice)
   Books/pamphlets___ Internet___ Software___ TV, newspaper, radio___ Library___ School___
   Teen/Recreation Centers___ Government Organizations___ Other_____

Thank you for your time and valuable opinions!

Figure 2. Survey Sample 2

Tucson-Pima Public Library
Public Libraries as Partners in Youth Development, a Wallace-Reader's Digest Funds Initiative
Staff Computer Service Questionnaire

Your input regarding the use of teen computer aides is needed in order for us to effectively evaluate this initiative. The teen computer aides at the Woods, Mission, Valencia and Main Libraries have been working with the public for approximately 8 months. This brief survey is to gather information on the effects of the teen computer aides on library staff. Thank you.

1. In what way have the teen computer aides increased your workload?
   _____

2. In what way have the teen computer aides decreased your workload?
   _____

3. In your opinion, what benefit have the teen computer aides been to your library?
   _____

4. Please include any observations or anecdotes that reflect benefits to staff provided by the teen computer aides.
   _____

Thank you for your cooperation

Figure 3. Survey Sample 3

Tucson Youth
Employment and Training Needs Survey Development Team

The Tucson Youth Job Training and Employment Coalition and the youth of Tucson would like your input regarding what the Tucson Community can do to provide teens with jobs and job training. A group of 6 youth from the Metropolitan Education Commission Youth Advisory Council/ Tucson Teen Congress, Tucson-Pima Public Library, Tucson Parks and Recreation, and the Tucson Pima Arts Council developed this brief survey so you can have your voices heard around jobs and job training. Please take a few minutes to complete this survey. Thank you.

Please tell us about yourself:

Age: ☐ Under 14 ☐ 14 ☐ 15 ☐ 16 ☐ 17 ☐ 18 ☐ 19 ☐ 20 ☐ 21 ☐ over 21

Gender: ☐ Male ☐ Female

Zip Code _____

Ethnicity:

☐ Asian ☐ African American ☐ Caucasian ☐ Hispanic ☐ Native American

Other (please indicate) _____

Will you be attending school in the fall? ☐ Yes ☐ No

What is the last grade you completed in school? ___

1. Have you ever had a job? ☐ Yes ☐ No

2. How many jobs have you had? ___

3. Do you have a job now? ☐ Yes ☐ No

4. If you answered yes to Question 3, are you satisfied with the job you have now? ☐ Yes ☐ No
   Why or Why not? _____.

5. Do you want a job? ☐ Yes ☐ No
   If yes, what kind of job do you want? _____

6. Are you looking for a job? ☐ Yes ☐ No

7. How long have you been looking for a job?_____

8. How many jobs have you applied for? _____

9. Of the jobs you applied for, how many jobs have you been hired for? _____

10. What do you think prevents you from getting the job you want? _____
    _____

11. Do you know where to find information about jobs for teens? ☐ Yes ☐ No

12. Do you know where to find information about job training for teens? ☐ Yes ☐ No

continued on next page

13. Where would you look for information about jobs? (Mark 1st, 2nd, 3rd choice)
Books/pamphlets ___   Internet ___   Software ___   TV, newspaper, radio ___   Library___
School ___   Teen/Recreation Centers ___   Government Organizations ___   Other ___

14. Who do you talk to about planning your career? (Mark 1st, 2nd, 3rd choice)
Self ___   Family ___   Friends ___   Librarian ___   School Counselor ___   Teacher ___
Adult You Respect ___   Someone working in the job ___   Other ___

15. How important do you feel it is to prepare for an interview?
☐ Important   ☐ Not Important   ☐ Don't Know

16. Do you have access to a computer? ☐ Yes   ☐ No

17. Do you have access to the Internet? ☐ Yes   ☐ No

18. What kind of transportation do you rely on?
☐ Walk   ☐ Bike   ☐ Bus   ☐ Bus Pass   ☐ Car   ☐ Parent   ☐ Other_____

19. Do you need childcare? ☐ Yes   ☐ No   ☐ Do not have a child

20. Do you have childcare? ☐ Yes   ☐ No

Tucson Youth Employment and Training Needs Survey Development Team
Daniel Medrano - Metropolitan Education Commission Youth Advisory Council/Tucson Teen
Congress, member of the Tucson-Pima Public Library youth advisory committee
Kyra Witten – Tucson Pima Arts Council
Leanna Leon – Tucson Pima Arts Council
Reuben Bravo – Tucson Parks and Recreation
Terransay Whaley – Tucson Parks and Recreation
Marcos Parra – Tucson Parks and Recreation

[1] *Information Power: Building Partnerships for Learning* (Chicago: ALA/AASL, 1998)

Ziarnik, Natalie Reif. *School and Public Libraries: Developing the Natural Alliance* (Chicago: ALA, 2003).

These two books discuss inter-institution collaboration and the value of work with colleagues to achieve library goals.

[2] Holt, Glen E. *Public Library Partnerships: Mission-driven tools for 21st century success.* (http://www.stiftung.bertelsmann.de/english/publika/download/index.htm). Bertelsmann Foundation.

This article is published by the Bertelsmann Foundation, International Network of Public Libraries in German and in English. It is the report of an international study of library partnerships.

[3] McCook, Kathleen de al Pena. *A Place at the Table: Participating in Community Building.* (Chicago: ALA, 2000).

McCook gives reasons, methods and examples of public library collaborations with the community's non profit and government organizations.

[4] Austin, James. *The Collaboration Challenge* (San Francisco: Jossey-Bass, 2000).

Austin discusses partnerships between business and non profit and government agencies from a business perspective. He identifies common elements and key strategies for collaborative success.

GETTING STARTED

Some partnerships are long term, some for a defined time period and some for the life of a specific project or funding cycle. The following are steps to making any type of partnership successful.

1. Find out about a potential partner. What is its mission? Who is the leader? How many staff members does the partner have? What is its budget? What are its strengths and weaknesses?

_____

_____

_____

_____

_____

_____

2. Identify what the partners have or do that will further your library's mission or improve your service.

_____

_____

_____

_____

_____

_____

3. Describe how you will collaborate. Include what each organization's role will be and what resources of each will be needed for success. Set goals and create a timeline of activities.

_____

_____

_____

_____

_____

_____

4. Determine who will be involved from each organization. How will your library and the partner organization(s) communicate? What happens if designated staff members leave the library or the partner organization?

_____

_____

_____

_____

_____

_____

5. How will you know that the partnership is working? If the partnership is ongoing, set up an annual progress review, or in the short term, know what you want to accomplish and how you will measure success. Make sure the partners agree to whatever assessments or evaluations you plan to make.

_____

_____

_____

_____

_____

_____

6. Obtain a letter of agreement, a contract, or an informal memo of agreement with partner organizations that includes agreement from the organization's director and key staff members.

_____

_____

_____

_____

_____

_____

PERFORMANCE MANAGEMENT AND EVALUATION

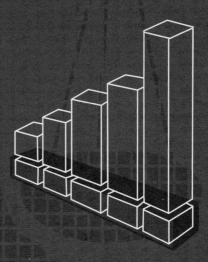

Measuring Library Success

How do you measure your library's success? Is it circulation numbers? Is it the number of patrons? Or the usage of your electronic databases? In a recent customer survey, EBSCO Publishing found that over 60 percent of its customers had no "formal" method for quantifiably tracking organizational success, and that over 50 percent used informal customer feedback as their primary success metric. This is interesting, as libraries are awash in statistical data. Librarians gather data by use (transactions), input (costs) and output (circulation, visitation), and they report this data to chief librarians, academic vice presidents, consortia partners, funding agencies and government organizations as a few examples.

Although there is an abundance of "data" in the library, knowledge of how to use this data to measure performance and demonstrate organizational impact and benefits is sometimes lacking. Writing about higher education, Steve Hiller and James Self state, "The wise use of data, information, and knowledge in planning, decision-making, and management can improve library performance. While libraries have long collected data...it is only recently that they have begun to use it effectively in library management."[1]

"What you measure is what you get." Managers leading a for-profit, government, or a library organization understand that their measurement system affects the behavior of their employees and the effectiveness of their business strategy.[2] As Robert Kaplan, a member of the Harvard Business School Faculty and an expert on performance management, states, "By quantifying and measuring the strategy, organizations reduce and eliminate ambiguity and confusion about objectives and methods. They gain coherence and focus in pursuit of their mission."[3] Quite simply - first the strategy needs to be clear; then the strategy needs to be linked to key measurable results that apply to the various groups within the organization. And, finally, the data needed for the "measurable results" must exist.[4]

Investing in a performance measurement system can be time intensive and culturally difficult; however, the benefits are tangible. For example, many successful libraries use their analysis and findings to facilitate fundraising and budget justification, communicate success and professionalism to constituencies (e.g. faculty, students), prove effectiveness and demand of resources, build usage enthusiasm by students and patrons, and distinguish their program or university among peers. Without clearly defined metrics there is no way to determine relative effectiveness in achieving the library's mission. This inability can have tremendous impact on many key operations, such as:

- The allocation of funds among programs and resources is difficult: there are no clear guidelines on spending money. Data relating to program effectiveness is insufficient.

- The communication of a library's impact on its constituency and community is intangible: a library is unable to communicate to its staff or its constituents that it is effective in achieving its goals and that its resource usage is efficient. This inability hinders funding efforts and overall marketing.

- Staff management can become ambiguous and reactive, rather than proactive: staff roles and objectives are not clearly tied to a strategy, so groups do not know with any clarity whether or not they are performing well.

MEASUREMENT INNOVATIONS: NEW TOOLS AND NEW APPLICATIONS OF OLD TOOLS

The need for libraries to be businesslike and accountable to boards, donors and society has generated innovative attempts to apply and develop new performance and impact tools for all types of libraries. Here are some examples:

Public Libraries: The U.S. National Commission on Libraries and Information Science (NCLIS) has worked since 1970 at "appraising,...strengthening the relevance...[and] promoting research and development for extending and improving library and information services for the American people."[5] This agency's newest major public library responsibility is to oversee a project to increase "the effectiveness of evaluation for improved public library decision-making and advocacy." Funded by the Institute for Museum and Library Services, the three-year study overseen by Professors John Carlo Bertot and Charles McClure at Florida State University, Information Institute, College of Information is centered on the new data-related issues of library management. The project abstract notes:

> Public libraries are under increasing pressure to show value, impact, benefits, quality, and other uses of their resources and services to the local communities that they serve. Being able to articulate library impact, value, quality, and other benefits can enable librarians and managers to demonstrate what public libraries do for their communities along a number of important dimensions, such as literacy (traditional, information, and technology), economic, and social factors. The need that this demonstration project addresses is: *How can "best practice" evaluation strategies support public librarians and managers demonstrate the value of their libraries to the communities that they serve?*[6]

> The wise use of data, information, and knowledge in planning, decision-making, and management can improve library performance.

Academic Libraries: In 1994, the Association for Research Libraries (ARL) adopted the New Measures Initiative. Hillier and Self describe the initiative this way:

> This initiative...inform[s] data collection that go[es] beyond traditional input/output measures to capture use and impact of libraries. In 1999 eight areas of interest were identified: user satisfaction, market penetration, ease and breadth of access, library impact on teaching and learning, library impact on research, cost effectiveness of library operations and services, library facilities and space, and organizational capacity.[7]

One of the new measurement tools that eventually emerged from this initiative is a service-quality assessment survey/analysis system called LibQUAL+[TM]. The website for this product explains its management purpose:

> LibQUAL+(TM) is a suite of services that libraries use to solicit, track, understand, and act upon users' opinions of service quality. These services are offered to the library

> The need for libraries to be businesslike and accountable to boards, donors and society has generated innovative attempts to apply and develop new performance and impact tools for all types of libraries.

community by the Association of Research Libraries (ARL). The program's centerpiece is a rigorously tested Web-based survey bundled with training that helps libraries assess and improve library services, change organizational culture, and market the library.[8]

School Libraries: There have been many school library and media center statistical studies in recent years. School accreditation is the force behind school activities in statistical gathering and analysis. Like public and university libraries, however, issues about performance and outcomes have become paramount in school management and evaluation. The recent publications of Dr. Keith Curry Lance and his colleagues at Colorado's Legislative Research Service illustrate the emphasis on libraries' and librarians' performance quality and outcomes. Titles include: "Powering Achievement: How School Librarians Impact Academic Achievement"; "Scientifically-Based Research on the Impact of School Libraries on Academic Achievement"; and "How School Librarians Help Kids Achieve Standards..."; and, finally, a study for Illinois, "How Powerful Libraries Make Powerful Learners."[9]

EVALUATING YOUR LIBRARY'S PERFORMANCE AND VALUE

If you are new to the measurement field, the following guidelines should make your start easier:

1. Clearly define your library's mission and strategic objectives. Measuring the accomplishment of these objectives will drive your data gathering and analysis.

2. Identify the most compelling ways in which your library impacts your community, and which audiences it serves with its programs and services.

3. Determine the types of information you will need in order to convince your audience of the library's value, e.g.:
   a. Anecdotal evidence, e.g. stories, quotations, letters
   b. Traditional library performance or output statistics
   c. Comparative data from peer libraries
   d. Cost benefit analysis
   e. Return on investment

4. What data collection methods will work best for you in your efforts?
   a. Telephone or online surveys of patrons, partners, employees.
   b. Focus groups comprised of patrons, partners, employees.
   c. Quantitative value collection from NCLIS and other sources, e.g.,
      the U. S. Census Bureau of Statistics, local telephone companies,
      and records of telephone calls and e-mails to other, similar libraries.
   d. Identification and/or calculation of statistical surrogates or
      loading factors with multivariate analyses.

5. How rigorous will the research methodology have to be to justify the information produced?

6. Does your library have the staff resources and expertise to gather that data?
   If not, how will you get those resources?

7. How will you communicate your findings to your constituencies:
   news articles, annual report, community meetings etc?

A good introductory essay that sets some groundwork for accessing your library's performance and determining its value to its community is "Demonstrating Impact," particularly the "Quantifying" pages, found at the WebJunction website. It has the additional asset of being updated often.[10] Visits to EBSCO Publishing's Customer Success Center will yield additional sources of analysis and helpful suggestions.

The success stories in this section also should help you get started. Each story in this section relates how a library has used statistics to measure, report, and/or plan its effective performance and value to various groups of constituents. The library staff at the University of Arizona at Tucson, for example, used its own research team to find the optimum basis for improving the quality of electronic document printing and handling e-document reserves – and saved money in the process.

Fort Worth (TX) Public Library used the PLA *Planning for Results* materials to evaluate and then to optimize technology purchases that immediately benefited users and influenced non-technology decisions in positive ways. King County (WA) conducted an institutional self study, including a statistically reliable customer survey and a formal analysis aided by consultants, and then developed a new strategic service development plan.

> Measuring the accomplishments of your library's objectives will drive your data gathering and analysis.

The Delaware Division of Libraries utilized Balanced Scorecard and Six Sigma, proven quality tools, to develop customer-centric measurements.

The Carnegie Library of Pittsburgh hired economists and other experts to estimate a dollar value of benefits as a return on investment from their system's services.

Like the other analyses included in the case studies in this section, the Carnegie Library study immediately became the basis for making changes in services and programs to increase the benefits that users receive. In each case, measurement evaluation became the basis for improved performance.

ENDNOTES

1   Steve Hiller and James Self, "From Measurement to Management: Using Data Wisely for Planning and Decision-Making," *Library Trends* 53, no. 1 (2004): 129-155, *Academic Search Premier*, EBSCO*host*, 21 Aug. 2006.

2   Robert S. Kaplan and David R. Norton, "The Balanced Scorecard: Measures That Drive Performance [cover story]," *Harvard Business Review* 83, no. 7/8 (2005): 172-180, *Business Source Corporate*, EBSCO*host*, 21 Aug. 2006.

3   Robert S. Kaplan, "Strategic Performance Measurement and Management in Nonprofit Organizations," *Nonprofit Management & Leadership* 11, no. 3 (2001): 354, *Business Source Corporate*, EBSCO*host*, 21 Aug. 2006.

4   Stratton Lloyd, Hannah Wu, and Karen Weigert, "Bringing Strategy to Life Through the Balanced Scorecard," <http://www.epnet.com/uploads/thisTopic-dbTopic-350.pdf> (unpublished thesis).

5   *U.S. National Commission on Libraries and Information Science*, 8 May 2006 <http://nclis.gov/>.

6   John Carlo Bertot and Charles McClure, "Increasing the Effectiveness of Evaluation for Improved Public Library Decision Making and Advocacy: Abstract," *US Institute of Museum and Library Services*, 8 May 2006 <http://www.ii.fsu.edu/projectFILES/IMLSEval/IMLSEvalApproaches.Abstract.Apr16.06.pdf>.

7   Hiller and Self.

8   *LibQUAL*, 7 May 2006 <http://www.libqual.org/>.

9   "School Library Impact Studies," *Library Research Service*, 8 May 2006 <http://www.lrs.org/impact.asp#colo>.

10 "Demonstrating Impact: Quantifying," *WebJunction*, 8 May 2006 <http://www.webjunction.org/do/DisplayContent?id=1203>.

"We really want to ensure that our buildings and services are in touch with what our patrons need, not solely what we feel they need. We want to be mindful of demographics, technology, and other societal factors."

Julie Wallace
Community Relations Manager
King County Library System

Challenges

• Incorporate patron needs into Library construction, renovation and service plans

Solutions

• Library teams planned, delivered, and analyzed the Patron Experience Transformation Project survey, with expert assistance from two consulting firms, the assistance of 80 staff members, and a project budget of $250,000

• A Library Discovery Team surveyed patrons and surpassed participation goals by 168 percent. In all, the survey reached an estimated 27 percent of the patron population

Benefits

• An implication study of survey results offered administrators a clear sight line to patrons and their needs

• Survey responses revealed a high level of patron loyalty and participation

• Library drafted the King County Library System Strategic Blueprint, an action plan to implement improvements

Overview

The King County Library System (KCLS) in Washington State is one of the largest circulating libraries in the United States. Situated near Seattle in the state's most populous county, it ranks as the second busiest system in the nation, with 43 branches circulating over 18 million items annually.

In 2005, KCLS initiated the Patron Experience Transformation Project, a comprehensive research project to survey user "habits, preferences and perceptions…in order to pursue its goal of continuous improvement of the patron experience."[1] With the expert assistance of two consulting firms, the assistance of 80 staff members, and a project budget of $250,000, library teams planned, delivered, and analyzed the survey to exacting standards, ensuring valid results.

Project analysis revealed a clear sight line to patrons, opportunities for improvement, and an affirmation of library-patron partnership. A resulting strategic blueprint for action now maps the library system's plans for enhancements to its 43 existing branches and construction of new branch buildings.

CHALLENGE

In 2004, KCLS inaugurated a new building program to expand library branches and patron services. It received a $172 million bond in 2004 to renovate the existing branches and build two new structures. According to King County Library System Community Relations Manager, Julie Wallace, incorporating patron needs into the ongoing construction plans is of paramount importance. "We really want to ensure that our buildings and services are in touch with what our patrons need, not solely what we feel they need. We want to be mindful of demographics, technology, and other societal factors."

While KCLS had an established history of conducting small library patron surveys, Wallace and the entire system's library administration recognized that a large-scale program warranted a broad surveying scope. These catalysts gave rise to the Patron Experience Transformation Project.

SOLUTION

In January 2005, the Patron Experience Transformation Project began with marketing research, including the discovery and design process. A research plan was proposed and approved in May and a sequence of qualitative and quantitative research studies occurred in June and July, 2005. Insights derived from the research would help the library system define its own "gold standard for patron experience."[2]

To guide them in the year-long process, KCLS planners hired advisors from the consulting firms of SLR Inc., and Fernow Consulting, who served as project managers. "Our selection of consultants was significant. Making sure we had the right people working with us was important," says Wallace. "We found that no single consulting firm could facilitate both project organization and survey structure, so we worked with two different consultants." Fernow Consulting helped design and field the survey, and SLR, Inc. provided the organizational guidance, staff training, and internal review processes.

Teams of library staff from across the system administered each phase of the project. Wallace emphasizes that deep involvement from KCLS management and staff was essential for project design, focus, and implementation. "We didn't want staff to feel we were talking to patrons to field negative feedback about them. It wasn't our objective." Each team attended a day-long project retreat, to train, plan, review results, or develop strategies and action items.

With guidance from Fernow Consulting, the Planning Team of 20 staff members conducted interviews with KCLS managers, a review of King County census data, a review of KCLS operational data, review of prior KCLS patron research, and numerous observational visits to KCLS branch libraries. The research team consulted relevant academic and managerial literature on customer satisfaction, customer service and library quality and developed a research model that encompassed Loyalty, Satisfaction, Service Quality, Library Practices, and Patron Awareness and Use.[3]

The team created the actual survey using Survey Monkey software, www.surveymonkey.com. It was designed to gather the following insights from current patrons:

- What is the profile of the KCLS patron population in terms of library habits and demographics?

- What are the levels of patron awareness and usage of library offerings?

- How well does KCLS perform in terms of patron satisfaction and loyalty?
- How well does KCLS perform in terms of various dimensions of library practices that are important to patrons; and, how well is KCLS delivering on them?
- What patron "segments" exist that might enable KCLS to better tailor its offerings to them?
- What cues can we find from other great customer experiences that might enhance KCLS?[4]

Survey questions fell into a classification of four categories:

1. People (patron segments)
2. Place (general library behaviors)
3. Price (quality, practices)
4. Promotion (satisfaction and loyalty)

Planners hoped to survey 3,200 individuals ages 14 and older, who, by their geography, gender, age, ethnic background, education levels, and varying proficiency levels in English created a comprehensive representation of the system's current patrons.

A Discovery Team of 40 non-management staff volunteered to deliver, or physically facilitate the survey process at all branches. Candidates for the Discovery Team required manager recommendations, and were screened by Chapple Langemack, managing librarian/staff project lead and Denise Siers, associate director for public services. Once chosen, the librarians administered surveys at branches other than their own, to eliminate bias from both librarian and patron.

To market project awareness among patrons prior to the survey start date, organizers posted informational materials in library branches and on the KCLS website.

Discovery Team members met with patron respondents one-on-one to introduce the survey and invite responses to online or paper survey formats. Respondents could complete the survey at a library branch, or at home. The time needed to complete the survey ranged from 20 to 30 minutes.

The Discovery Team reached a respondent base of 5,404 individuals; and in so doing surpassed expectations by 168 percent. In all, an estimated 20,000 KCLS patrons were approached for the survey, an estimated 27 percent of the patron population. The response data was accumulated in an online database and downloaded for analysis by the research team.[5]

The $250,000 budget for the Patron Experience Transformation Project covered fees for both consulting firms and funded wages for library staff who substituted for team members involved in the survey delivery process.

BENEFITS

An implication study of the results offered administrators a clear sight line to patrons, and revealed a high level of patron loyalty. "We know from past surveys that our library system receives high satisfaction ratings from patrons," says Siers. "However, this recent study showed us a level and patron loyalty and participation we'd never seen before – a deep sense of partnership with the Library. In fact, it is so strong that the teams decided to forever abandon the term 'customer' when referring to library patrons."

The study also revealed two areas of opportunity:

- Continue to build awareness of library system products and services.

- Improve the functionality of access to information. This opportunity includes enhancing physical space, clarifying policies relating to noise levels in various library areas, and reassessing the holds system.[6]

In 2006, a team of 75 library employees drafted the KCLS Strategic Blueprint, an action plan to implement improvements in the targeted areas. One action item for 2006-2007 is the Way-Finding Project. Using strategic displays, arrangements, and sign postings, it will guide patrons through the library system's physical structures and resources. As a consequence, KCLS hopes to cultivate highly-adept patron users who will take full advantage of library services, and guide others.[7]

Wallace and Siers report that KCLS will conduct a new survey in 2007 to track data against the baseline it has established.

What recommendations do KCLS library managers have for other libraries? "Our system's large scale is geographically and financially unique," says Siers. "This kind of program truly requires professionals to conduct a marketing survey with valid responses and evaluate the results." She continues, saying, "Even with outside consultancies, libraries of any size should deliver the survey with their own staff. High levels of communication and staff involvement are also essential for any successful library survey program."

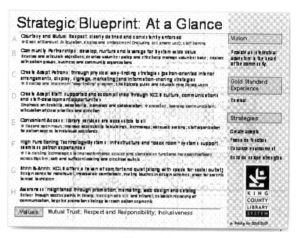

Figure 1.
King County Library System
"Strategic Blueprint"

ENDNOTES

1   Executive Summary, Patron Experience Transformation Project, page 1; King Country Library System

2   Ibid.

3   Executive Summary, Patron Experience Transformation Project, page 2; King Country Library System

4   Ibid.

5   Ibid.

6   Executive Summary, Patron Experience Transformation Project, page 1; King Country Library

7   Executive Summary, Patron Experience Transformation Project, page 1; King Country Library System; Strategic Blueprint, King County Library Systems.

"The 'Planning for Results' process helped us make technology choices that are most beneficial to customers…The concept of evaluating what you're doing now and what you're going to drop is hard for public libraries. That's why we loved this process."

Deborah C. Duke
Collection Management Administrator
Fort Worth Public Library

Challenges

- Local library is required to submit a technology plan to the state library organization

- Library's technology was antiquated and slow

- Library staff possessed limited technology skills

- Increase the Library's identity within the community

Solutions

- Formed a cross-functional team to evaluate the Library's technology and develop a plan for the future

- Utilized Diane Mayo's Technology for Results as road map for their review process

- Gathered extensive input and feedback regarding the Library's technology supported services (TSSs)

- Scored technology needs based on multiple factors to determine priorities

Benefits

- After 5 months, the Library had a comprehensive road map of technology enhancements & a prioritized "shopping list" to enhance library services

- Top priority technology purchases were made & patrons began to benefit immediately

- Technology planning process resulted in confident choices by the committee & influenced other decisions across the library

- Cross functional participation built stronger ties across library & city organizations

OVERVIEW

The Fort Worth Public Library (FWPL) experienced a "good news" story that got even better. In 2005, in honor of the tenth anniversary of The Fort Worth Public Library Foundation, the Library received substantial funding to enhance its obsolete technology. This 21st-century update positioned library staff to reconsider their methods of current technology management and focus on moving forward. The exciting addition of these new resources, coupled with the Texas State Library's requirement that public libraries submit long range plans that included technology, launched FWPL's new technology planning process.

A committee was formed in August of 2005 and over the next four months, using the Public Library Association's 2005 guide, *Technology for Results: Developing Service-Based Plans*[1], authored by Diane Mayo, they developed a comprehensive three-year technology plan aimed at supporting the Library's critical services, staying focused on emerging technologies, and increasing benefits for the 661,000 residents served by 15 library facilities across the Fort Worth area.

Challenge

Deborah Duke, collection management administrator at the Fort Worth Public Library, remembers what it was like before the library received their technology upgrade in 2005. "Staff members would have to apologize to the public (for the lacking equipment)." The Fort Worth Public Library Foundation helped fund a new integrated library system (ILS). The new ILS required other technology upgrades, including replacement of 500 out-dated staff and public personal computers, an overhaul of the library's network, including T1 lines to all branches, new servers, increased security, technology training for library staff, and employee access to the City's network.

It quickly became obvious that the Fort Worth Public Library couldn't stop there. Both the city and the state required the Library to submit a technology plan for the future. The Library's recently developed long range service plan had revealed gaps not only in the technological infrastructure, but in knowledge, expertise, and planning as well. They needed a technology plan to satisfy these various requirements and avoid finding themselves in a position of "apologizing" in the years to come.

Solutions

In August of 2005, a 15-member committee was formed that included library staff members, Library Advisory Board and Foundation members, City IT representatives, and a technology consultant from the North Texas Regional Library System. PLA's Technology for Results was chosen as the committee's road map. "The 'planning for results' process worked very well for us," reports Duke. "(The process) helped us make technology choices that are most beneficial to customers…The concept of evaluating what you're doing now and what you're going to drop is hard for public libraries. That's why we loved this process."

After reviewing the business imperatives of their task, the committee spoke to other library staff members, administrators, and consultants. They gathered feedback and ideas about existing and potential technology-supported services (TSSs), and collected information to understand the requirements and costs of these services. This myriad of ideas and information was then compiled for the committee to review into one big spreadsheet, also known as "The Sifter." Much of their two-hour biweekly meetings were spent reviewing and scoring various technology ideas within The Sifter, looking at all possible technology directions and weighting them based on multiple factors.

The factors considered were:
- Is the service existing or new?
- Does the service support public or staff/administrative activities?
- Are there business imperatives (such as City Council goals) requiring the service?
- Cost estimate
- Impact on IT/Computer Services staff time
- Required staff training
- Impact on other staff's (non-IT) time
- Relation to library business plan performance targets
- Audience appeal

Technology for Results recommended many of the factors the committee used, but Duke notes, "We added elements such as measuring each item against the City's goals to make sure the Library is in line with the City Council's long-term objectives."

The Sifter proved a very valuable tool for the committee's technology planning efforts. "It makes you really think about how each technology service impacts the library patrons and our staff, " reports Deborah. "It also helped prepare us for the additional information we needed to gather."

The technology plan was then developed based on scores from The Sifter and considerations about technology enhancements which might be invisible to the public, but essential for the Library to improve and run effectively. The final plan was submitted to the Advisory Board, and presented to The Foundation in January, 2006, outlining the Library's technology direction for fiscal years 2006, 2007, and 2008. The planning committee decided to remain intact and now meets quarterly to check progress and adjust plans as necessary. "We were sure we had missed other technologies we could have considered," says Deborah. "But we're still learning and we realize the plan has to be flexible (to accommodate new ideas)." Items they'd like to consider for the future include downloadable audio books, RFID, and productivity software for the library staff.

BENEFITS

Staff members at the Fort Worth Public Library are confident that patrons are already benefiting from their enhanced technology. For one thing, the lines for PCs are shorter because the computers now operate faster and people can get their work done quicker. These benefits will only increase as implementation of the technology plan continues. Envisionware® software now being installed will help the Library manage public computer use. Usage data will then be analyzed to check plans and priorities for the next fiscal year. Other purchases and projects outlined for the immediate future include assisted listening devices and ADA compliant workstations, self checkout stations, summer reading software, library blogs, and online signup for library classes.

Participating in the process and utilizing Technology for Results proved an educational experience for the committee's members. They felt confident in their decisions and were able to use The Sifter data to influence other decisions across the Library. Involving participants from the Library Advisory Board, The Foundation, and the City's IT Department built stronger ties with those organizations. The Library now has a prioritized shopping list for The Foundation and its Friends organization. Most importantly, it has a manageable and doable technology road map for enhancing the Library's future. Concludes Duke, "A plan isn't truly successful until it turns into reality."

ENDNOTES

[1]   Diane Mayo. *Technology for Results: Developing Service-Based Plans*. Chicago, IL: Public Library Association, 2005.

CASE STUDY: CARNEGIE LIBRARY OF PITTSBURGH, PITTSBURGH, PA

"Everyone loves the Library, but they don't necessarily understand the Library's overall relationship with the community. This (Community Impacts and Benefits) Report gives us a way to talk to the community about the importance of the Library."

Dr. Barbara Mistick
Director
Carnegie Library of Pittsburgh

Challenges

• Compensate for statewide funding cuts to libraries

• Prepare for pending state congressional vote on library funding

• Increase awareness of the Library's economic value to the community, state officials, community representatives, and corporate leaders

• Refute the popular assumption that the Library is well-funded because of its famous name

• Seek public relations assistance to validate and communicate the Library's mission and value

Solutions

• Commissioned the Center for Economic Development at Carnegie Mellon University to conduct an economic impact study regarding the Library's impact to the regional economy

• The study examines the Library's value in terms of Return on Investment and overall contribution to the community

• The study employed a conservative, academic approach to assessing the Library's impact

• The Library hired a local public relations firm to assist in disseminating information from the report

Benefits

• Authenticated the importance of Carnegie Library of Pittsburgh throughout the region, particularly among young people and families

• Built awareness of the Library with elected officials, community leaders, grant providers, and potential donors

• Gathered extensive feedback from the community regarding the services patrons value most

• Defined clear, unbiased metrics on a full scale of impacts the Library has on the community

Overview

Despite its 110-year presence in the region, Carnegie Library of Pittsburgh (CLP) struggled to articulate its contribution to state and local leaders during recent statewide funding inquiries. In order to quantify its impact and overall value, the Library commissioned an independent study to explore the effects its services and programs have on the community. The resulting report provided clear metrics on a variety of economic and social impacts the Library has on the region. Employing this third party, academic approach, CLP was able to authenticate its importance for the region's residents, elected officials, community leaders, and potential donors, and increase awareness of the Library's value as a provider of funded services and programs.

Challenge

Although Carnegie Library of Pittsburgh encompasses 19 separate locations hosting more than two million visitors annually, the Library's FY2005 budget shrank to FY2002 levels as a result of state funding cuts. Dr. Barbara Mistick, director of Carnegie Library of Pittsburgh, points out, "We had to cut service hours because of the reduced funding." With a critical state vote scheduled for July of 2006, the Library was facing political challenges that could further reduce funding. The Library leadership knew it had to take action.

"Everyone loves the Library, but they don't necessarily understand the Library's overall relationship with the community," explains Dr. Mistick. "We continue to work on our capital improvements program. We're renovating, rejuvenating, and relocating our system. But when we talked to state officials, they had no sense that the Library was important as far as economic development. We weren't even on their radar screen. We weren't seen as an economic player for elected officials, or community or corporate leaders," she emphasizes.

Lynn Seay, principal at PRwerks, a public relations firm the Library hired to help shape its position in the community, further articulates the challenge. "The Library needed to clearly articulate its value – to inform the community and pressure state government. People assume the Library is well-funded because of the Carnegie name," she says.

Solutions

To quantify the Library's value, CLP commissioned the Center for Economic Development at Carnegie Mellon University in the fall of 2005, to conduct an economic impact study by analyzing the Library's impact on the regional economy. The report, made public in April of 2006, examines both the Library's value to the economy in terms of return on investment as well as its contributions to people and their communities.[1]

"We did not have a budget for the study," admits Dr. Mistick. "Fortunately, we were able to obtain $40,000 from the ALCOA Foundation and the Eden Hall Foundation to fund the project."

Defining and Explaining the Economic Impacts

The study's design relied on a model known as IMPLAN. According to Jerry Paytas, Ph.D., director of the Center for Economic Development, "IMPLAN is a common model used for impact analysis. It traces the flow of economic activity from a national to a local level. If you spend one dollar in this sector, where does it go? We looked at many different aspects, from the construction and renovations to the Library's purchasing. We looked at locations near the Library and how the location of the Library impacts where people spend," he explains.

Overall, the study encompassed four levels of economic impact:

Direct Impacts = Spending by the Library and its customers
Indirect Impacts = Purchases of supplies and materials by vendors to the Library
Induced Impacts = Purchases by households and other industries as a result of increased incomes from the direct and indirect impacts
Output = the total value of goods and services produced by an economy[2]

Figure 1. Employment Impact

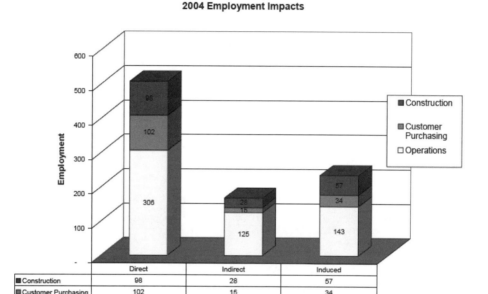

2004 Employment Impacts

	Direct	Indirect	Induced
Construction	98	28	57
Customer Purchasing	102	15	34
Operations	306	125	143

Gathering customer input was also a critical element used to build the study. To accomplish this, Dr. Paytas and his team incorporated focus groups and a patron survey into their research. Key Library stakeholders attended the focus groups and more than 1,300 individuals completed the survey, available both in print and online. The 25-question survey asked responders about the features and benefits of their local library branch, as well as the services they utilize at the Library and within the surrounding community. "The Library had quite a bit of involvement," notes Dr. Paytas. "Library staff would select people at random to take the survey so we could get the best representative sample. And we tapped a lot of the Library's data regarding cardholders and attendance. The Library had an incredible amount of information about their operations."

The survey results yielded key insights regarding the Library's contribution to people and their communities. For example, 63 percent of the survey respondents listed the availability of computers as a major benefit, with one third reporting use of the offered electronic databases. Eighty-eight percent of respondents indicated that they access the Library's website remotely. When asked what more could the Library do, customer responses included offer longer hours, more materials, and more of the kinds of programs already offered.[3]

Figure 2. Library Contribution to Community[4]

Table 8: Community Benefits Identified by Survey Respondents

Question 9: In your opinion, what benefits does your library branch currently provide to the surrounding community?	Major Benefit (Number of Responses[5])
Promote literacy and learning	982
Improve neighborhood quality of life	940
Provide activities for children and teens	876
Informal gathering place	792
Provide career and job resources	750
Public meeting rooms	596
Provide resources for business	572
Attract customers to other businesses	479
Increase property values	457
Increase safety	433

When asked about Carnegie Mellon's contribution, Dr. Mistick offers, "They were able to take a conservative, academic approach to substantiating our impact. They helped us by recommending what should be in the study and the information that should be featured. We learned the Library could substantiate an economic impact, such as the value of the 300 community meetings we hosted last year, or the value of books and databases. University analysts were able to draw a parallel to the databases we purchase and what it would cost the community to buy those separately." She adds, "Some of these things we knew, but we couldn't articulate them in this way. With this level of third party validation, the report becomes a very powerful tool."

Communicating Results

At the conclusion of the study, the Library hired PRwerks to help disseminate the report information. "PRwerks has broadened our vision as to how to share this information," reports Dr. Mistick. "The firm had experience working with ballot referendum issues, so they were a good fit for us." With the company's assistance, key metrics from the report were communicated throughout the region. Report results were featured on local radio and television stations, as well as in editorial sections of local newspapers. Dr. Mistick adds, "This study helped the Post-Gazette write an opinion piece about the importance of the Library, and has given our customers information they can use when they contact their senators and state representatives."

Report Highlights

- Carnegie Library of Pittsburgh is the area's most visited regional asset.
- In 2004, Carnegie Library of Pittsburgh supported more than 900 jobs and $80 million in economic output in Allegheny County, through its operations and renovations.
- The Library provides an economic benefit of $3 for every dollar it spends.
- For every dollar provided by the City of Pittsburgh and the Allegheny Regional Asset District, the Library provides more than $6 worth of benefits.
- The Library provides more than $75 worth of benefits per capita for residents of the County.
- Despite the interruption of major neighborhood library renovations, and reductions in operating hours, the hourly circulation of material increased 28 percent system-wide from 2002 to 2005.[5]

Benefits

The publication of the economic impact study has yielded many pleasant surprises: one out of every five regional residents holds a library card, including 70 percent of Pittsburgh residents between the ages of 13 and 36, and 42 percent between 0 and 12. Dr. Mistick reports, "People are looking at the Library in a different way since the numbers about young users were published. This has authenticated the importance of the Library in the community."

Staff members have also gained a greater understanding of their customers and the community's needs and expectations. "Increased safety was a Top 10 item for benefits of the Library. People have an informal place to come and meet. It brings people out. Communities that have social capital and engagement with each other have less crime," adds Dr. Mistick.

Even Dr. Paytas admits there were unexpected results in the report. "Customer spending was higher than I thought it would be. And market share was a surprise, particularly when we looked at Library visitors compared to sports event attendees and newspaper subscribers," he says.

Dr. Mistick concludes, "You can see the impact of the report already. Several community partners have come and done stories about the Library, including the local television station. Our elected officials are more aware of the Library and its role in the community, and grant providers have renewed confidence from what they've read. Some people will still want to support the Library because of their emotional connection, but this information will make other donors more informed. This (Community Impacts and Benefits) report gives us a way to talk to the community about the importance of the Library. When people hear it from a credible third party source, they hear the information differently."

And, yes, the state did vote to increase library funding in July of 2006; undoubtedly the report on the Carnegie Library of Pittsburgh's Impact and Benefits was a substantial influence.

Endnotes

[1]   Carnegie Mellon University, Center for Economic Development, "Carnegie Library of Pittsburgh Community Impact and Benefits," February 2006, p 1.

[2]   Ibid, p. 7.

[3]   Ibid, p. 18.

[4]   Ibid, p. 17.

[5]   Ibid, p. 2.

Case Study: University of Arizona, Tucson, AZ

"We needed to remove duplication of document delivery and management operations and streamline them into one centralized area. It was a learning experience to apply the Systems Analysis Approach to our needs. It helped us clearly identify problems and look at them from the customer's point of view."

Cheryl Neal
Library Specialist
University of Arizona Libraries

Challenges

• Improve quality of electronic document printing

• Improve quality of e-reserves technology

• Improve efficiency of operations for Document Delivery staff and equipment

Solutions

• Formed an expert team to study challenges of merging document delivery operations

• Identified solutions and plan of action using Systems Analysis Approach

• Purchased new e-reserves scanning products to update and streamline operations

• Streamlined technology and staff operations to improve document quality and service for users

• Quantified solutions and feedback with surveys

Benefits

• High acceptance rate among faculty and students for posting and managing course reserves

• Students pushing faculty to use new technology to manage course reserves

• Library staff cross-training in all service areas

• Saved $8,000 in student salary

• Reduced staff needed by one FTE with improved service

Overview

The University of Arizona Libraries staff adopted a systems analysis approach to assess and then modify its electronic delivery systems. The team developed a plan that merged the work activities of its Electronic Reserves, Interlibrary Loan (ILL) and Document Delivery units.

The team's plan and unique charge gave it the flexibility and autonomy to go from analysis to implementation in a short period of time. As a result, its work eliminated redundant operations, created new reserve services, improved document quality for users, reduced costs by $8,000 and allowed the team to return 1.0 FTE library specialist to the Library for other strategic/customer efforts.

The team's efforts are exemplified by the successful implementation of streaming audio and color graphic reserves, the merging of scanning and paging processes, and the system-wide implementation of ILLiad, OCLC's electronic Interlibrary Loan software program. University Library Specialist Cheryl Neal comments saying, "It was quite a learning experience to use the Systems Analysis Approach to merging document operations. It helped us clearly identify problems and look at them from the customer's point of view."

Challenge

This project began when students and faculty using the University of Arizona Library remotely reported an inability to print electronic documents. The main challenge was that existing library document-delivery technology used incompatible optical character recognition for Adobe formats. That issue provided the impetus for the creation of the Electronic Delivery Analysis Team (EDAT), a broadly representative library staff committee, to assess the Libraries' entire scanning and printing operation, including ILL. Spearheading the effort were Library Specialist Cheryl Neal, Library Specialist Ellen Knight, and Jeanne Voyles, the team leader of the Library's Document Delivery Team.

The second challenge became time. Originally, EDAT was to do its work within a year. That shrank to a window of six months when Dean of Libraries Carla Stoffle responded to an opportunity to apply for University grant money. The grant would pay for EDAT recommendations if the whole project could be completed before the end of the fiscal year. That gave EDAT six months. "We were on a short timeline," remembers Cheryl Neal. "We had to analyze areas of interest, research and propose innovative solutions to reduce duplicated operations, including storage and technology, then take two or three weeks to interview vendors and make purchasing decisions, all by the end of the fiscal year."

Solution

At the outset, the Library's Cabinet, which includes the Dean of Libraries, gave the team a unique charge – the flexibility and autonomy to go from analysis to implementation in a short period of time. Neal says the decision tapped member strengths. "Individual efforts and staff talents came to the forefront as time went on. Their combined experience and diverse perspectives helped us figure out what was needed." EDAT's preliminary assessment revealed that staff and technology were duplicating operations in several areas, making the department workflow inefficient. EDAT members decided to look at the Library's whole scanning and printing operation as a system. One aspect of this "System Analysis Approach," as the team came to call their method of problem solving, was an assumption that technology solutions existed that would improve customer service and operating efficiencies at the same time.

Systems Analysis Approach – EDAT's Systems Analysis Approach was centered on studying how well library system components worked and interacted. The phases of the approach were:

1. **Problem Analysis:** Identified specific problems, such as duplication of work in different areas.

2. **Requirements Analysis:** Identified the desired characteristics of a new system, such as using shared software across multiple services.

3. **Decision Analysis:** Based on analysis of data, recommended possible solutions.

4. **Implementation & Integration:** Implemented best solution, and integrated into existing processes.

The team also built into its mission the ability to make decisions within the immediate group during each phase of analysis. This gave members ownership of the decision-making process as department experts and helped save time. EDAT met twice each week, spending up to two hours each time assessing information, then formulating and assigning tasks to individual members or pairs. Informed by analysis, their action plan took shape, with four key requirements:

1. Streamline print stations and staff areas, from seven stations to four.

2. Restructure staff; rewrite job descriptions.

3. Execute an intricate training plan from pilot to full rollout to cross-train staff and users in the successful use of changed functions.

4. Implement scheduling and merge scanning stations to accommodate demand and centralized operations.

One of the EDAT leaders summarized the transformation this way. "We needed to remove duplication of scanning and printing operations and merge them into one centralized area, with consistent hardware and software applications. Scanners and staff stations were in different areas, some equipment was only lightly used, because the technology was out of date. We also needed to make sure that one central location was staffed and available at all times."

To meet that goal, the library licensed Docutek, an electronic reserves product that allows faculty to manage their own course material reserves. The license takes the burden off in-house developers to create a solution from scratch. Other purchases include Helix, a server for streaming audio, and several scanners. A grant of $25,000 secured from the University of Arizona's Technology Department covered these purchases.

Neal, Knight, and Voyles then launched a pilot study of the proposed solutions in the Science, English, Music, and Architecture departments. According to Knight, the test proved valuable for quality feedback. "We had a full semester of piloting the new setup. Department focus groups gave us feedback through an extensive ARL LibQual™ survey that gathers data about the quality of instructions, programs and services furnished by different campus units."

The solutions performed extremely well in the pilot study, and were implemented for the entire campus following a detailed communication plan. The Library web home page served as the main hub for putting the word out to campus, supplemented by e-mails to department liaisons, memos to Deans, Directors, and Department Heads, and advertisements in school papers and newsletters.

BENEFITS

Results couldn't be better. According to Ellen Knight, "Everything has been going very smoothly. The merging of staff talents for group learning, analysis, and production made this project successful." In addition to streamlining and the $8,000 cost savings, there is broad acceptance of the changes by the Library's customers – faculty and students. "The faculty loves it," she adds. "They love the freedom, the ability to archive and create their own course reserves. Students like the audio reserves; they don't have to come on campus to listen to selections for music classes. This gives them greater freedom beyond the Library's limited hours."

If past is prelude, the University of Arizona Libraries team expects faculty instructors to continue to manage course reserves, and to edit their materials using Docutek E-reserves. "Student demand should motivate them to do that, as instructors tell us that students call and ask them to put things on e-reserves. This should push faculty who haven't used the new system, to do so," says Knight.

Library staff training is another priority, the goal being to have everyone trained to service all four ILL and document delivery system areas. And because the team is always learning and improving, there will be a focus on improving the turnaround time required for the ILL borrowing process. Surveys showed them that 80% of users want a 72-hour turnaround time. They're implementing yet another new process to accomplish that.

Their advice to others facing a project of this scope? Cheryl Neal speaks for the whole team saying, "Spend the time to review the project's charge, and put together a strong, diverse project team with a good project manager. Tap everyone's talents. Merging of talent made this project so successful."

"Customer service is more than just a hand shake and a smile.
Libraries need to know they have their processes in place
so their service outcomes can be guaranteed."

Anne Norman
Director/State Librarian
Delaware Division of Libraries

Challenges

- Delaware libraries lag well behind other states in key service areas: 37th in Visits per capita, 45th in Reference Transactions per capita, and 29th in Circulation per capita

- Delaware libraries had misaligned strategies in dealing with statistical data, and no consistent repository for combining statistical library data

- Gathered measures were used for operational evaluation, but not strategic planning

- State wanted to improve their scores in Baldridge Award criteria – 45 percent of which focuses on results

Solutions

- Launched a comprehensive plan to improve the service of Delaware libraries

- Developed a new Vision and Mission for the state's libraries to "have library service that is second to none in the nation!"

- Developed a statewide plan using the Balanced Scorecard method of strategic planning and Six Sigma quality tools for process improvement

- Utilized the Balanced Scorecard and Insight Vision Software to compile library statistical data and focus metrics on strategic, customer-focused plans

Benefits

- Library employees across the state embraced the quality, customer-focused approach

- Developed a framework for understanding current library performance and planning for improvements

- Using the Balanced Scorecard provided clear focus for setting objectives in the service areas needing most improvement

- State and local library employees are now equipped with quality tools and training to set process improvements on the right track

OVERVIEW

The Delaware Division of Libraries (DDL) has a success story in progress and on track for a productive future. In 2002, DDL staff recognized that Delaware possessed low national rankings in key library service areas when compared to other states. Also suffering from low assessments on the Baldridge Award criteria, this state-level library development organization decided to take action.

Working with a team of consultants, the DDL launched the "Twenty Years Forward" plan to improve its rankings. The plan outlines the major findings hampering the state's library system and has introduced a systematic, quality-based approach to planning for improvement. Employing the Balanced Scorecard method of strategic planning and Six Sigma quality tools for process improvement, the DDL has developed an effective framework for understanding the system's current shortcomings, consistently measuring results, and planning customer-focused improvements to project the "First State" to "first in the nation in providing public library service."[1]

CHALLENGE

"We started on this journey four years ago," reports Anne Norman, director and state librarian for the State of Delaware's Division of Libraries. When 2002 national rankings revealed Delaware libraries as lagging behind in key service areas, such as 37th in library visits per capita, 45th in reference transactions per capita, 29th in circulation per capita, and 41st in staff expenditures per capita of public libraries, the state knew it was time to act.

The state's recent Baldridge Award assessment had also revealed shortcomings. "Of the seven areas examined within the Baldridge Award, 'Results' is worth the most – 450 out of 1,000 points," reports Despina Wilson, a management analyst II at DDL. "Our results in this category indicated that we lacked a systematic way of analyzing results. We have lots of data, but there's not a lot of rhyme or reason about what it tells us."

With this wake-up call, it was time to help the state's libraries transition from operational measures, data snapshots confirming current realities, to strategic measures – using library statistics to form correlations and set goals for future improvements.

SOLUTIONS

The joint consulting team of Himmel & Wilson Library Consultants and PROVIDENCE Associates, Inc. was hired to conduct a comprehensive study of Delaware's libraries and assist in the state's plan for the future. The team decided to take a "yellow brick road approach," says Norman. "We had to start at the beginning; take a snapshot of where we were regarding staff, collections, everything. We had to gather the baseline measures so we could set clear goals and objectives." In addition to the Baldridge Criteria, the team chose two unique tools to begin planning for improvements: Balanced Scorecard and Six Sigma.

What is the Balanced Scorecard?

Developed by Robert S. Kaplan and David P. Norton of the Harvard Business School, the Balanced Scorecard (BSC) is a holistic performance measurement system that links the short and long term activities of an organization with their vision, mission, and strategy using measurable goals.[2] What makes this tool unique is the measurement of different "perspectives" – Customer, Internal Processes, Knowledge/Growth, and Financial, with the measurable feedback from the customer being most important. As Delaware's Norman and Wilson shared in a recent ALA presentation, the Balanced Scorecard "is about aligning what we say and do, and provides focus on how to achieve the ultimate vision." Wilson also explains "Our scorecard includes the current state and the objective for each measurement. It shows the trends and gives us targets for achieving better results."

What is Six Sigma?

Six Sigma is a customer-focused process improvement methodology aimed at 99.99966% error-free work. The core of Six Sigma is about training and empowering frontline employees to recognize what's most important to customers, then measure and improve processes to make sure those customer requirements are met. In Delaware, local library administrators have been involved since the beginning, receiving training, presentations, and a firm foundation in process improvement.

The DDL team drew their initial measures from many sources, including extensive customer input through surveys and phone interviews. "We're using operational measures as output," reports Wilson. "We're now synthesizing those raw measures to come up with new measures to help us in other areas."

Compiling these massive amounts of data proved a challenge, as well, until the group identified Insight-Vision Software. This product had the capacity, the formatting, and the charts they were looking for, as well as the possibility of incorporating vendor data in the future.

BENEFITS

Armed with these powerful tools, the Delaware Division of Libraries is confident they're on the right track to improve state-wide library results and move closer to their new vision of "library service that is second to none in the nation!" They now have a solid method for frequently reviewing key metrics and the libraries' service trends. As Norman points out, "Looking at these numbers once per year is not enough. They need review at least quarterly, if not monthly." Wilson adds, "The Balanced Scorecard has become our planning document. We're at a state now where we've pulled everything out of the closet."

By fall of 2006, they plan to have a clear measurements template for all state public libraries. Via site visits, the DDL team will review each library's numbers with administrators, show comparisons versus other Delaware libraries, and assist local organizations in the areas where they'd like to focus. Eventually, they would like to see scorecards built for each library staff person and used in conjunction with the performance evaluation. Given the quality training employees have received to date, this will reinforce their role in improving customer service and improving processes.

Wilson, Norman, and colleague Theresa del Tufo have chronicled the Delaware Division of Libraries' journey in a new book with an anticipated publication date of 2007, from McFarland Publishers. The work will outline their steps to link Baldridge criteria and the Balanced Scorecard to their service plan. It will also provide recommended reading, Baldridge criteria, and library examples. They hope other states and libraries will benefit from their learnings in the process.

Anne Norman clearly endorses the measurement approach when she states, "Customer service is more than just a handshake and a smile. Libraries need to know they have their processes in place so their service outcomes can be guaranteed."

Figure 1.

Delaware Division of Libraries' Balanced Scorecard Framework

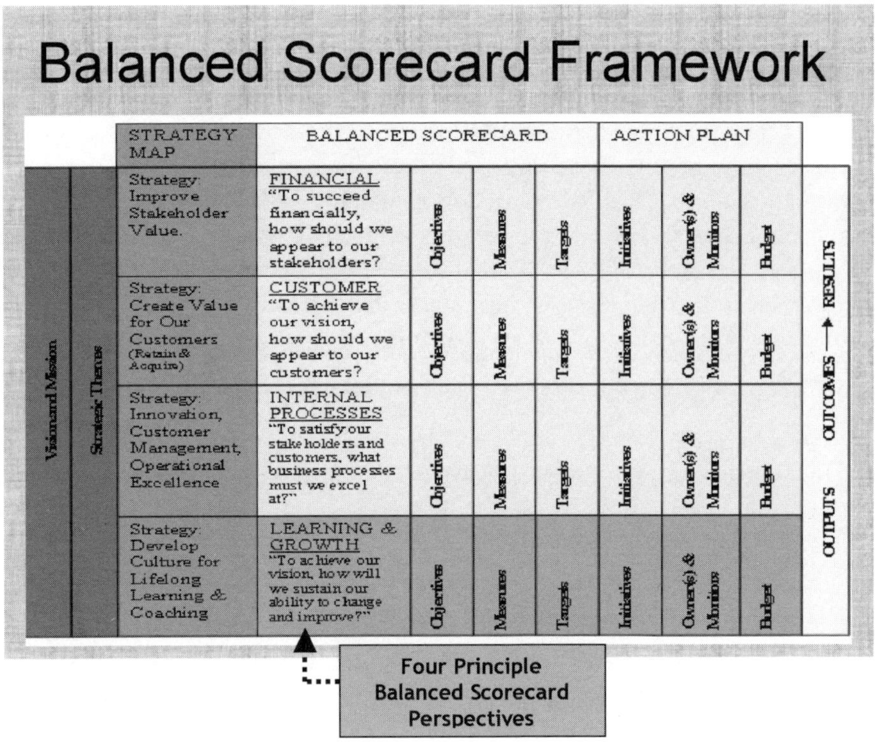

Figure 2.

InsightVision Software organizes Division of Libraries' data for principle scorecard metrics

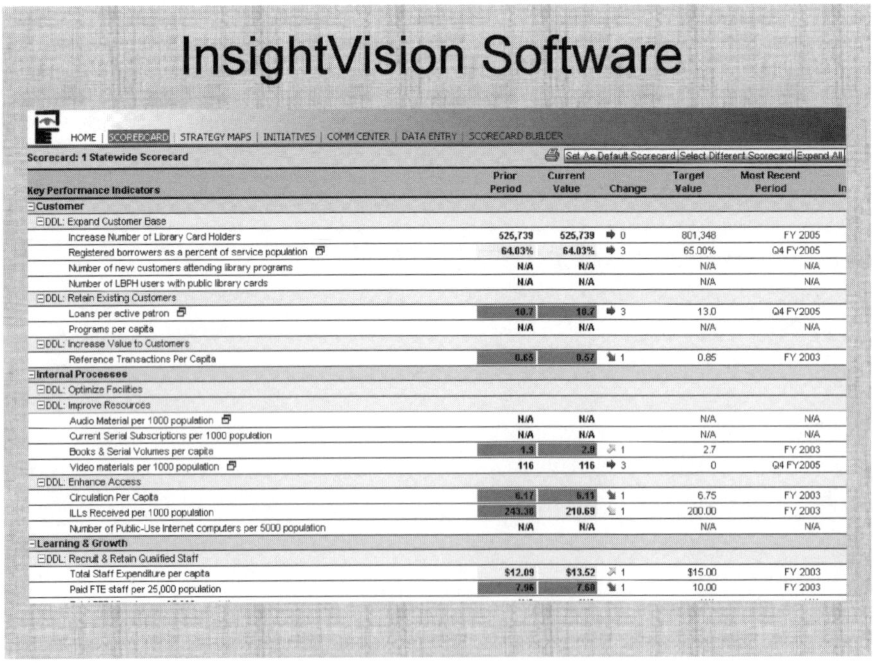

ENDNOTES

1   Himmel & Wilson, Library Consultants/PROVIDENCE Associates, Incorporated, "Twenty Years Forward: A Statewide Library Services and Construction Infrastructure for Delaware Libraries – Executive Summary."

2   Stratton Lloyd, "Building Library Success Using the Balanced Scorecard."
http://www.epnet.com/uploads/thisTopic-dbTopic-350.pdf

RECOMMENDED READING FOR STRATEGIC MANAGEMENT

The Balanced Scorecard: Translating Strategy into Action; by Kaplan, Robert, and Norton, David P.; Harvard Business School Press; September 1996; ISBN: 0875846513

The Strategy-Focused Organization; How Balanced Scorecard Companies Thrive in the New Business Environment; by Kaplan, Robert, and Norton, David P.; Harvard Business School Press (September 2000; ISBN: 1578512506

Strategy Maps: Converting Intangible Assets into Tangible Outcomes, by Kaplan, Robert, and Norton, David P., Harvard Business School Press February 2, 2004; ISBN: 1591391342

RECOMMENDED READING FOR ORGANIZATIONAL ALIGNMENT

Alignment, by Kaplan, Robert, and Norton, David P., Harvard Business School Press, April 24, 2006; ISBN: 1591396905

[1] *New Directives, New Directions: Documenting Outcomes* (www.imls.gov/applications/basics.shtm). Institute of Museum and Library Service.

This publication provides definitions, examples and a bibliography on using outcome evaluation. While specific for IMLS grants, it gives good information for anyone who is beginning to use outcomes.

[2] *Search for Schools, Colleges and Libraries.* (www.nces.ed.gov).
National Center for Educational Statistics-NCES

Library Statistics Cooperative Program. (www.nclis.gov/survey,htm).
National Commission on Libraries and Information Science-NCLIS.

These websites provide statistics on specific libraries as well as statistical summaries by type of library.

[3] Durrance, Joan and Karen Fisher. *How Libraries and Librarians Help People: A Guide to Developing User-Centered Outcomes.* (Chicago: ALA, 2005)

This book gives purpose, structure and techniques for libraries wishing to use outcome evaluation. It is about public library projects, but much of the information will be useful in any library setting.

[4] Hernon, Peter and Robert Dugan. *Action Plan for Outcomes Assessment in Your Library* (Chicago: ALA, 2002)

This book addresses both learning and research outcomes particularly for academic libraries.

[5] Rubin, Rhea. *Demonstrating Results.* (Chicago: ALA, 2005)

Part of the PLA "Results" series, Rubin focuses on how to conduct outcome evaluation.

GETTING STARTED

Librarians often assess and evaluate programs and services informally, and libraries have been collecting statistics for the past 100 years. In the current climate, libraries are asked to be more formal in their evaluations and more thoughtful in their use of statistics. Here are some steps to follow to move to this more sophisticated level of evaluation and measurement:

1. Decide on the scope of evaluation. Do you want to evaluate the library as a whole, or a specific service or particular program?

    _____

    _____

    _____

    _____

    _____

    _____

2. Brainstorm several ways in which you can carry out the evaluation you are planning. You may want to use more than one kind of evaluation for larger projects, but select the simplest way to do the evaluation that will get the information you need.

    _____

    _____

    _____

    _____

    _____

    _____

3. Will the evaluation technique and specific data collection instrument you want to use accurately measure the library activities you are evaluating?

    _____

    _____

    _____

    _____

    _____

    _____

4. If you are using surveys, interviews or focus groups, are the questions you ask clear and easy for those involved to answer? Pre-testing questions on a small group similar to those who will give you information will help to ensure that your questions are clear.

_____

_____

_____

_____

_____

_____

5. Determine what staff skills you will need to do your evaluation project. Will you need assistance from consultants or statisticians? Where will you get this help?

_____

_____

_____

_____

_____

_____

6. After you have collected data, how will you use the information? To whom will you report your conclusions based on the data collected?

_____

_____

_____

_____

_____

_____

ABOUT THE CONTRIBUTORS

Dr. Glen Holt is a writer and researcher for Holt Consulting. He has published widely. He is a regular columnist on library economics in *The Bottom Line* for Emerald Press, and for the new and innovative electronic journal, *LLN (Library Leadership Network) Bulletin*. He also serves as editor of *Public Library Quarterly* for Haworth Press.

Dr. Holt is the winner of PLA's Charlie Robinson Award (2003) for library innovation and risk taking. He was one of only thirty library professionals in the world to be named an "International Networker" for the Bertelsmann Foundation's International Network of Public Librarians from 1998 until 2003. He was director of St. Louis Public Library from 1987 to 2004. Dr. Holt holds an undergraduate degree from Baker University and a doctorate degree from the University of Chicago.

Dr. Leslie Edmonds Holt is President of Holt Consulting, advising not-for-profit organizations. She is also the associate editor of *Public Library Quarterly*. Dr. Edmonds Holt serves as a policy analyst and evaluator of After School Programs for ARCHS (St. Louis Area Resources for Community of Human Services), and for Provident Counseling Services. Dr. Edmonds Holt is a past president of the Association of Library Service for Children (ALSC), and is the recipient of the Carroll Preston Baber Award from the American Library Association, to support her research on how children use both online and card catalogs in public libraries.

Dr. Edmonds Holt was Director of Youth Services and Community Relations at the St. Louis Public Library from 1990 to 2004. Previously, she taught at the Graduate School of Library and Information Science at the University of Illinois at Urbana-Champaign. She has been a consultant and trainer for libraries and book publishers on reading and programs for children. She holds an undergraduate degree in history and secondary education from Cornell College, a graduate degree in Library Science from the University of Chicago, and a doctorate degree in Curriculum and Reading from Loyola University of Chicago.

Stratton Lloyd, Vice President of Customer Satisfaction and Medical Market Development, EBSCO Publishing, manages Customer Support, Expert Services, Training and Education, and Customer Success for EBSCO Publishing's customers. He was integral in the creation of the EBSCO Publishing Customer Success Initiative, whose mission is to create and deliver value-added offerings to help ensure the success of EBSCO customers (www.epnet.com/thisTopic.php?marketID=20&topicID=204).

He has worked with academic, junior college, public, elementary, medical and corporate libraries globally on a variety of technology, general management and product training engagements. Mr. Lloyd has more than 10 years of not-for-profit education and technology industry experience. He holds an undergraduate degree from Yale University and a graduate degree in Business Administration from Harvard University.

Kathleen A. Luz, Customer Success Specialist, is a managing editor, writer, and training facilitator for the EBSCO Publishing Customer Success Initiative. She creates and manages content for the company's online Customer Success Center, applying professional expertise in the fields of public relations, education, and publishing. Ms. Luz holds an undergraduate degree from Wellesley College and a graduate certificate in publishing from Emerson College.

Emily Hayden, Manager of Customer Success, has overall responsibility for EBSCO Publishing's Customer Success Initiative, managing training, communication, and support of EBSCO Publishing customers world-wide. She has nearly 20 years of experience in customer satisfaction and process improvement and is a certified Master Black Belt in Six Sigma methodology. Ms. Hayden is a graduate of the University of Michigan.

Nancy E. Veiga, Senior Technical Writer, creates customer-focused documentation and online help for EBSCO Publishing's Customer Satisfaction Group. Ms. Veiga has over 15 years' experience writing for a variety of industries, including taxation, health care and database publishing, as well as several years of sales support and project management in the telecommunications industry. She holds an undergraduate degree from Bentley College and a Masters in Technical and Professional Writing from Northeastern University.

Marcie Brown is EBSCO Publishing's Training Resources Manager, as well as Customer Service Communications Manager. Ms. Brown is responsible for product training including development of instructional tutorials and online training courses. She writes extensively for the company's support site and authors announcements and communications to customers worldwide. She has ten years of management experience, including over two years in Human Resources.